Portals

Releasing the Power and
Presence of God into the Earth

by
Dr. Patti Amsden

*Portals: Releasing the Power and Presence
of God into the Earth*

ISBN 1-931527-70-9

Patti Amsden Ministry
1203 Vandalia
Collinsville, Illinois 62234
Phone: 618-345-4224, Ext. 109
www.pattiamsden.org

cover design
Odell Mitchell III
Third In Line Productions
thirdinlineproductions@hotmail.com

iii

"Dr. Patti Amsden uniquely combines academic excellence with the operation of the spirit of revelation! This book will make a much-need contribution to one of the most pressing issues facing the body of Christ, i.e. how to scripturally engage in spiritual warfare. This volume gives insights I have not found anywhere else, and it will release victory in you and your ministry."

Rev. Jim Hodges
President and Overseer,
Federation of Ministers and International Churches
International

"After reading Portals: Releasing the Power and Presence of God into the Earth, you will have witnessed an extremely unique gift from God. Dr. Patti Amsden beautifully weds revelation from the Word with application for your life! As a theologian and scholar, her insights will remind you of the revelation Apostle Paul so often taught. As a practitioner and leader, her insights will remind you of the wisdom Apostle James so often demonstrated. This book will inspire, excite, and instruct all those who read it!"

Rev. Hope Taylor
Director, International Leadership Embassy of Washington
D.C.

"The prophetic insight and theological understanding contained in this book are earth shattering! That is exactly what the Father intended. Now is the time and this is the hour for the church to arise and to welcome the King of Glory through Portals. Thank you, Dr. Patti, for releasing the revelation and scriptural understanding of these age-abiding doors. This book is a must for intercessors."

James Nesbit
Director, Prepare the Way
Ministries International

ACKNOWLEDGMENTS

I would like to thank the people whose loving efforts and proficient skills helped in the publication of this book:

First, those who assisted in the editing process: Dallas Amsden, Pastor David Amsden, Lee Ann Conner, Heather Galloway, Brad and Pamela Greer, Deedra Mager, and Dawn Stark. I am grateful for the time that they invested, the encouragement that they instilled, and the detailed consideration that they gave to my words.

Secondly, the layout and format consultant: Deedra Mager. I am thankful for the long hours that she spent at the computer and for her willingness to use her expertise to bring excellence and beauty to the work.

Thirdly, my administrative assistant: Pamela Greer. I am indebted to her for all the proficiency and structure that she brings to every aspect of my ministry and for all the publication details of which she took oversight to bring this book to print.

Fourthly, the book cover designer: Odell Mitchell, III. I am appreciative of his willingness to use his college training to produce a cover that visually communicates the words contained within the pages.

Finally, the support team: My husband, my children and their spouses, and my grandchildren, and my father. I am deeply grateful for a spouse and family who would allow me the freedom to dedicate long hours in study and writing.   Their encouragement and devotion strengthened me at every stage of development.

TABLE OF CONTENTS

INTRODUCTION

How spectacular are the places where God appears! Heaven resounds with the multi-layered worship of angelic beings as well as redeemed humanity who stand engulfed in the glory and splendor that emanates from the Most High God. His presence enraptures. His beauty engulfs. His person enthralls and evokes a response. "Holy, Holy, Holy," the seraphim resonate. "Worthy to receive honor and glory and blessing," ten thousand times ten thousand, and thousands of thousands reverberate. God appears in His eternal dwelling and all of Heaven adores.

The psalmist cried, *"How lovely is your dwelling place, O Lord Almighty. My soul yearns, even faints, for the courts of the Lord; my heart and my flesh cry out for the living God."* (Ps. 84:1-2, NIV) He loved the earthly place where God appeared in His glory. The thought of meeting with God and experiencing the presence of God produced a deep longing and a fervent emotion within his whole being. His memories of the splendor of God's attendance created a desire to make the altar of God his dwelling place.

In every generation, believers long to experience the glory of God while they are alive. This book on portals recounts the experiences of many that had dynamic, personal encounters with the Living God. Not only are their experiences explored, but also the principles and patterns by which Heaven can be accessed are defined. Portals are pathways between the earthly realm and the spiritual realm. Portals are points where Heaven and earth converge. At portals, believers experience the phenomenon of Heaven released into the earth.

Within the context of this book, the word heaven will appear in two ways. When heaven appears with a capitol H, the realm under discussion will be the abode of God, the highest Heaven. When heaven appears with a lower case h, the realm under consideration will be man's heaven, which was placed under man's authority in the original dominion mandate given to Adam.

Also note the use of the term 'man' and the referencing pronoun 'his' will be used throughout the book predominantly to identify mankind, both male and female. At various points the word 'man' will apply to only the male gender, but the contextual usage should suffice to provide the reader with clarity of application.

CHAPTER ONE

Adam: The Mandate to Keep an Open Heaven

Living Under An Open Heaven

What an amazing existence Adam must have experienced! The Bible gives some explanation of the glories of Eden, which was a perfect environment for man and a welcoming atmosphere for God. Man and his surroundings were in perfect harmony. Man and his God were in perfect fellowship. Wow! Scarcely can the mind comprehend the blissful state into which Adam and Eve were welcomed into the earth.

Scripture tells us that God formed man from the dirt. The word formed (*yatsar* in the Hebrew) means to mold or squeeze into shape. The idea is best communicated by visualizing the process in which a potter would place a lump of clay upon his wheel and, through applying pressure with his hands, transform the earth into a finished piece of pottery. God molded Adam to be an earthly reflection of God's own image. Hand-crafted! Personally sculpted! Perfectly formed! What a specimen of beauty Adam must have been!

With a body formed from the dust of the earth, Adam was well-suited to his world. Adam and Eve were placed in an environment specifically engineered by God to sustain and promote physical life. They would be fed from that which the earth produced. They would labor within the physical creation to tend, manage, and develop the world over which God had given them dominion. (Gen. 1:26-28; Ps. 8) The earth would respond to its lords. Surrounding them was beauty and bounty from which they would eat, with which they would labor, and of which they would take pleasure. Provisionally, it was plentiful! Aesthetically, it was appealing! Environmentally, it was inexhaustible!

After God had formed Adam's body, He breathed His breath into Adam causing the clay vessel to become a living soul. Whereas Adam's earthen body harmonized with his earthly environment, the act of God imparting His breath caused Adam's soul to harmonize with Heaven's environment. Adam and Eve were suited to spiritual life. They walked with God and talked with God. They enjoyed unbroken fellowship with Him who is Love. They partook of flawless instruction from the Master who is Truth. They experienced the glory of the One who is Light. Heaven was open to the earth, and Adam and Eve lived in the glories of it.

One could say that Adam and Eve lived under an open Heaven. They enjoyed the realities in both the physical and spiritual dimensions. The Heavenly or spiritual reality was accessible, unveiled, and knowable to them. They were equally at home in God's manifest glory as in the physical home called the Garden of Eden. Likewise, God did not keep His realm distant from Adam's realm. God walked in the Garden and spoke to Adam as a Father to a son. The Scripture gives God's plan for man in the Genesis story, which was that man and God would dwell together without separation, division, or distance. God would freely access the earth and man would freely access an open Heaven.

Building A Heaven-Filled Earth

God not only elected to make man in His image, but God gave man the task of working in the Heaven-filled earth. Adam and Eve were to take the raw elements that were abundant in creation and further develop the earth. The dominion mandate of Genesis was not just to keep the earth tidy and status quo. God told them to be fruitful and fill up the earth. (Gen. 1:28) The command for fruitfulness was not limited to only natural procreation. Man was given the task of transfiguring the world from its perfect beginning into a mature creation.

Even a cursory glance at the Bible reveals that Scripture opens with a garden and closes with a city. Something happens between Genesis 1 and Revelation 22. Earth, which was created good, has been changed. Man has been at work. Man has been progressively restructuring the earth. Man has been transfiguring the world through various stages of development until the glories of the immature Edenic world are reworked into the matured glories of the New Jerusalem.

Being told what to do is not the same thing as being told how to do it. Adam and his heirs would need a schematic. They would need to follow the example set down for them by the Father who formed the visible world from a pattern already set in the invisible world. *"Through faith we understand that the worlds were framed by the Word of God, so that things which are seen were not made of things which do appear."* (Heb. 11:3) The invisible is the model for the visible. Heaven provides the blueprint for the earth.

What should each stage of the reconstruction reveal? Heaven on earth! What should each new rebuilding disclose? Heaven on earth! What should every modernization unveil? Heaven on earth! Such was the assignment given to the heirs of God – that of building Heavenly replicas into all spheres of earthly existence. As a result of such re-creative actions, God would continue to freely access the earth and man would continue to freely access an open Heaven.

Building an Open Heaven

That which Adam was commissioned to build was an earthly copy of Heaven. How Adam should build was likewise clearly defined. He was to follow God's pattern. Genesis 1:1 reveals that, *"In the beginning God created the heaven and the earth."* The next verses explain that God took six days to form the earth. The six-day pattern used by God outlines a guide for man's reconstructive labors. (For the context of this manuscript, only three days of the six-day pattern will be discussed.)

God's Day One: Genesis 1:3-5: *"And God said, Let there be light: and there was light. And God saw the light, that it was good: and God divided the light from the darkness. And God called the light Day, and the darkness he called Night. And the evening and the morning were the first day."*

On day one, light was generated into the earthly realm. The source of the light was not natural because the sun, moon, and stars were not created until day four. Therefore, it is reasonable to assume that a revelation or a manifestation of God, Himself, was the source of light. This is consistent with many passages where God is referred to as light and the giver of light. (Ps. 18:28; I Jn. 1:5; Rev. 21:23; 22:5)

An important principle emerges. The arrangement that would follow after day one would not only be created in the light of Heaven, but it would be specifically designed to reveal Heaven's light. Light, or a special manifestation of God moved into the new emerging creation. All that came after – the land, seas, animals, skies, stars – would be developed to make known some aspect of God. The creation would testify to the Creator. The seen would unveil the Unseen. The observable would undrape the Invisible.

Psalm 19 confirms that creation tells the story of God's glory. Every aspect was engineered to illustrate, demonstrate, and communicate the eternal in the realm of the temporal. On day one, God breaks into the darkness to reveal Himself in the created order. Light dawns.

<u>God's Day Two</u>: Genesis 1:6-8: *"And God said, Let there be a firmament in the midst of the waters, and let it divide· the waters from the waters. And God made the firmament, and divided the waters which were under the firmament from the waters which were above the firmament: and it was so. And God called the firmament Heaven. And the evening and the morning were the second day."*

On day two, God set up the firmament. The Hebrew word for firmament, *raqiya*, means expanse and is based upon the root *raqa*, which means to make broad, to stretch out, beat out, or flatten out. The biblical imagery created by the use of the word *raqiya* is that of a tinsmith beating a piece of metal until it is flattened into a sheet. That sheet or shell surface is then cast over the earth. By placing the shell in the heaven, God was in essence pitching a tent over the earth. Why would God place a tent or tabernacle in the sky? This scripture gives at least two explanations.

First, the shell provided a dividing point between the waters under it from the waters above it. The waters under the tent constituted the vapor canopy pre-Noah's flood and the clouds in the sky post-Noah. The ground waters, such as the lakes, seas, and rivers, are also part of the waters below the firmament. The waters on the upper side of the firmament are described in the Bible as a crystal sea that is before the throne of God. (Rev. 4:6; 15:2) Several times people in the Scriptures were given the opportunity to see the water that was on the topside of the firmament shell.

The elders in Moses' day got to glimpse through the temporarily transparent shell. They saw God seated and under His feet was a clear pavement that was declared to look like a sapphire stone, which was the Bible's pictorial way of describing the Heavenly waters called the crystal sea. (Ex. 24:9-11) Ezekiel was also allowed to view the waters on the top of the firmament tent. He likewise described the crystal sea as a sapphire stone. (Ez. 10:1)

The firmament was a boundary between God's Heaven and man's heaven. Originally, all the waters had been the same waters collected in the same location; but on day two, God separated the waters by the shell. The waters on each side were, nonetheless, identical. A further explanation of the nature of those waters will follow in chapter four; but at this point in the text, the important issue is that the waters under the canopy were identical to the waters above. Apart from anything happening that would cause a change in the created order, Adam's heaven was reflective of God's Heaven.

Secondly, all earthly tabernacles are built as dwelling places for God or the god to whom the tabernacle is dedicated. A tabernacle is a place of divine presence. Moses was told to build a tabernacle and, upon completion, God's presence was manifest. (Ex. 40:33-38) In Solomon's tabernacle, God's glory again appeared. (II Chr. 5:13-14) The Highest Heaven is God's habitation. There He appears in glory and sits enthroned in majesty. By erecting the firmament, God was disclosing His intent that man's heaven should be a place of God's appearing just as was His own Heaven.

Psalm 19:4-5 metaphorically confirms the idea of God's tabernacle among men by describing how the sun (symbolic of light and glory) makes an appearance in the sky. Verse four even states that God has *"set a tabernacle for the sun"* in the firmament. The imagery is unmistakable. Just as the sun's glory shines down from the natural sky over man, God's intent is that His glory would shine down from the spiritual sky over man. Man's heaven was to be a duplication of Heaven and thus a dwelling place for God. On day two, God rebuilt His habitation in man's heaven.

God's Day Three: Genesis 1:9-13: *"And God said, Let the waters under the heaven be gathered together unto one place, and let the dry land appear: and it was so. And God called the dry land Earth; and the gathering together of the waters called he Seas: and God saw that it was good. And God said, Let the earth bring forth grass, the herb yielding seed, and the fruit tree yielding fruit after his kind, whose seed is in itself, upon the earth: and it was so.   And the earth brought forth grass, and herb yielding seed after his kind, and the tree yielding fruit, whose seed was in itself, after his kind: and God saw that it was good.   And the evening and the morning were the third day."*

On day three, land appeared and with it all the vegetation that grows out of the ground.   Once man's heaven was structured, man's earth could be arranged. Orderly arrangement in the earth followed orderly establishment in the heaven. The earth is made to respond to heaven.

Even today, the vegetation of the earth grows during seasons of a warm heaven and lies dormant during times of cold air. The sun and rain from the sky bring forth fruitfulness, while the lack of either causes damage to the productivity of the ground.   Earth was created to act in response to times, seasons, climates, or other heavenly mandates. Should the sun be cut off, the earth would die. The natural communicates the spiritual.   Man's earth will only be prosperous when man's heaven is properly ordered.

Building By Another Pattern

<u>Adam's Day One</u>:   Genesis 1:24-28: *"And God said, Let the earth bring forth the living creature after his kind, cattle, and creeping thing, and beast of the earth after his kind: and it was so. And God made the beast of the earth after his kind, and cattle after their kind, and every thing that creepeth upon the earth after his kind: and God saw that it was good. And God said, Let us make man in our image, after our likeness: and let them have dominion over the fish of the sea, and over the fowl of the air, and over the cattle, and over all the earth, and over every creeping thing that creepeth upon the earth. So God created man in his own image, in the image of God created he him; male and female created he them. And God blessed them, and God said unto them, Be fruitful, and multiply, and replenish the earth, and subdue it: and have dominion over the fish of the sea, and over the fowl of the air, and over every living thing that moveth upon the earth."*

Adam and Eve's first day was God's last workday, day six. Man was created along with all the land animals over which he would rule and which he would utilize in his dominion task. One could say that the lights came on for

Adam on his first day. He was given the light of life and he was illuminated as to his earthly assignment. Day one is always the dawning of the light.

On day one, light from Heaven breaks into the earth to show some aspect of the unseen. God determines to reveal more of His glory, divulge another of His secrets, or proclaim a new phase of His plan. He sends light from above. If man will receive the light, walk in the light, and reflect the light, then Heaven will be made known in earth.

Because God is the source of light, day one always comes as a result of His initiative. He is always causative. Man's activities in the earth result from God's prior action. "*Let us make man,*" God determined and then acted. Examples abound. It was God's idea to anoint David to be king, arrest Moses at the burning bush, call the disciples to follow Christ, and knock Saul off his horse. God stirred the Babylonians to come against Israel, set aside Cyrus to fund the rebuilding of the temple, and caused Nebuchadnezzar to go mad in order that he might recognize the God of the Israelites. Scripture reveals that Jew and Gentiles alike were subjects of divine light. And, once the light dawns, the responsibility to build becomes man's.

Light shined upon Adam. He viewed the garden. He identified the animals. He beheld his wife. Above all, He saw his likeness to God. He heard his mandate to rule. He tuned in to the promise of fruitful earth. He listened as God forbade Him to eat of the tree. Above all, He discerned the voice of his Maker. Light penetrated. He knew what to do; and if he walked in the light, God would be glorified in Adam's realm.

Adam's Day Two: Genesis 3:1-7: *"Now the serpent was more subtle than any beast of the field which the Lord God had made. And he said unto the woman, Yea, hath God said, Ye shall not eat of every tree of the garden? And the woman said unto the serpent, We may eat of the fruit of the trees of the garden: But of the fruit of the tree which is in the midst of the garden, God hath said, Ye shall not eat of it, neither shall ye touch it, lest ye die. And the serpent said unto the woman, Ye shall not surely die: For God doth know that in the day ye eat thereof, then your eyes shall be opened, and ye shall be as gods, knowing good and evil. And when the woman saw that the tree was good for food, and that it was pleasant to the eyes, and a tree to be desired to make one wise, she took of the fruit thereof, and did eat,*

and gave also unto her husband with her; and he did eat.
And the eyes of them both were opened, and they knew that
they were naked; and they sewed fig leaves together, and
made themselves aprons."

If Adam's day one was God's day six, then Adam's day two would have occurred simultaneously with God's day seven. In Scripture, day seven is a Sabbath or a day of rest. God had finished His creation on day six and, therefore, had entered His Sabbath rest. (Ex. 20:11) Adam's day two was God's day of rest. If God was resting, Adam should have been resting. If God was taking His Sabbath, Adam should have spent the day reposing and enjoying all the works of God.

Day two should have been a day of adoration, affirmation, and adulation of the sovereignty of God. The first couple should have rendered praise for the inheritance that God's labor had provided. Worship is an act that affirms and acknowledges that which is worth the highest honor. Worship testifies to that which takes priority, holds utmost value, and possesses the preeminent importance. Adam and Eve should have spent their day two in the worship of God. Thanksgiving is a rendering of praise and an affirmation of dependence upon someone else. No one thanks himself. Rather, thanksgiving is a conscious act of gratitude given to the one who has bestowed a gift. Adam and Eve should have spent the Sabbath giving thanks for their endowment.

If they had done so, they would have fulfilled the day two requirement. They would have erected a worship-firmament or a firmament-tabernacle. A glimpse into the Heavenly scene reveals that the angels never cease to offer praise. (Is. 6:1-3; Rev. 5:11-12) Worship is tabernacle activity. Thanksgiving and praise is the response of beings enraptured by God's presence. Had Adam and Eve worshipped, they would have followed God's re-creative pattern and established their heaven as the abode of God.

Adam and Eve failed the worship assignment. They failed to be thankful. They looked at what had been withheld (the fruit of one tree) rather than the bounty that had been bestowed. They ascribed worth to the word of the serpent above the Word of the Lord. Rather than the contrite act of self-submission, they exalted their own desires and will above God's decreed Word. They failed to worship on day two. Hence, they did not pitch a tabernacle for God's glory. They did not enthrone God upon their praises. They did not order their heaven after the pattern of God's Heaven.

Although they did not pitch a firmament-tabernacle for God, they did set up a firmament. They gave worth to the serpent. They adored his plan. They praised his idea. They offered worship to another god. In so doing, they dedicated their heaven to be enthroned, inhabited, occupied by the serpent and the fallen angels who surround his being. Man's sphere, both his heaven and his earth, was designed to reflect God's glory. Adam was mandated to keep the area under his management aligned with its original purpose. He failed. His heaven was altered. Correspondingly, his earth would respond to the new satanic arrangement enthroned in man's heaven.

Adam's Day Three: Genesis 3:17-19: *"And unto Adam he said, Because thou hast hearkened unto the voice of thy wife, and hast eaten of the tree, of which I commanded thee, saying, Thou shalt not eat of it: cursed is the ground for thy sake; in sorrow shalt thou eat of it all the days of thy life; Thorns also and thistles shall it bring forth to thee; and thou shalt eat the herb of the field; In the sweat of thy face shalt thou eat bread, till thou return unto the ground;*

for out of it wast thou taken: for dust thou art, and unto dust shalt thou return."

Following the creation pattern which God had established, Adam and Eve's third day was the day to build the earth. Having structured heaven on day two, man was to follow God's lead and begin to restructure the earth. A properly structured heaven would release a new heavenly work in the earth. The three-day pattern was originally to be: revelation, then worship, then work. Or, the three-day pattern could be defined as illumination, then adoration, then formation. Day two activity precipitates the success or failure of day three.

Adam and Eve failed the day two assignment. They failed to worship God. They failed to erect a firmament-tabernacle to house God in their heaven. They perverted the heaven; hence, the earth would reflect the skewed condition. No longer could the earth manifest the glory and life of a godly Heaven. It would bring forth thorns. Earthly labors would no longer be a walk through paradise.

Closing the Heaven

Eden, which had formerly been a perfect environment for man and a welcoming atmosphere for God had been radically altered. The change in the heaven immediately affected the earth. First, God had formed a body for Adam that was perfectly suited and connected to the earthly environment. After his rebellion, the dust of his body reflected the same distorted condition as the dirt of the ground. Fleshly thorns of disease would be experienced in the dust of Adam's body just like thorns and thistles would be present in the dust of the ground. Eventually, the curse would win and the body would return to the dust.

Secondly, God had breathed into Adam causing him to be perfectly suited and connected to God's environment. Adam had not used his breath to worship. He had not breathed out fellowship, thus fellowship was severed. He had not spoken truth, therefore truth eluded him. He had not praised God's glory, hence he lost his glory. Adam and Eve were naked. They lost the covering of light and glory that had been their garment. They were disfellowshipped, disinherited, and disrobed.

Thirdly, God's original firmament-tabernacle had provided an open heaven. Adam and Eve closed the

Heaven. They set up a strange firmament, pitched a different sort of tabernacle, constructed a perverse canopy. This counter-tabernacle sealed off access to God's Heaven by erecting a barrier. They would no longer enjoy the reality of the Heavenly dimension. God's presence and His glory became veiled, closed, shut away. Adam and Eve were no longer free to access the open Heaven. To further reinforce the reality of their new condition, they were cast out of the garden; and angels were set to guard the way back to God's presence.

God's design, which was for man and God to dwell together without separation, division, or distance, was inoperative. God no longer had free access to the earth and man no longer had free access to an open Heaven. Heaven was no longer on the earth. Heaven was closed.

CHAPTER TWO

Abraham: The Practice of Building Altars

Passing the Worship Test

Living under a sealed-up Heaven, metaphorically affirmed by the sealed-off Garden of Eden, would present new challenges for all followers of God. In spite of the new environment, God would require the same actions from anyone who would obey Him as He required of the first couple. Adam and Eve had failed the worship test, thus disqualifying themselves from ruling the heaven and managing the earth for God. Future 'adams' would all be called to worship. How well they would comply with their worship directive would determine the effectiveness of their earthly dominion assignment.

God did not recall His commission upon humanity when Adam fell. God's decreed purposes remained the same. People who would bear His image as sons and rule the earth as vice-regents was still God's design for mankind. Therefore, God set about to restore His plan by appointing a new race of 'adams.'

Genesis 12:1-3, 7: *"Now the Lord had said unto Abram, Get thee out of thy country, and from thy kindred, and from thy father's house, unto a land that I will shew thee: And I will make of thee a great nation, and I will bless thee, and make thy name great; and thou shalt be a blessing: And I will bless them that bless thee, and curse him that curseth thee: and in thee shall all families of the earth be blessed. . . . And the Lord appeared unto Abram, and said, Unto thy seed will I give this land: and there builded he an altar unto the Lord, who appeared unto him."*

One could call Abram (whose name God later changed to Abraham) a replacement 'adam.' After all, he would become a father, a progenitor, or a fountain-head of a nation and would be a blessing to all families of the earth, which result would have followed the first Adam had he not become the fountainhead of transgression. Abraham was also given the promise of land. Although this passage does not specifically mandate Abraham to take dominion, nevertheless dominion is implied because property ownership requires stewardship.

God's call upon Abraham could be likened unto a day one. Light dawned. God separated the darkness of the patriarch's country and family when He spoke, "*Get thee out*." What would be Abraham's response? What kind of a firmament-canopy would he erect? Would he set up a worship tabernacle? Genesis 12 tells us that he built an altar to the Lord.

If Abraham's call was his metaphoric day one, then one could expand the symbolism to imply that raising an altar was his day two. As has already been discussed, the worship offered on day two sets forth a tabernacle or firmament-heaven under which man will dwell. On Abraham's second day, he passed the worship test when he built an altar to the Lord.

Offering Acceptable Worship

Altars are places where worship is offered. How altars are to be made, where they are to be placed, how they are to be used, and who can approach them are all carefully outlined within the pages of Scripture. They are God-ordained and God-controlled. In setting about to restore His plan and purpose for man to fellowship with Him and to rule the earth for Him, God instituted altars.

Altars are points of contact. They are places where 'adams' worship and draw near to God. They are places where offerings and gifts are brought to God in a show of adoration, honor, and thanksgiving. Various kinds of gifts were placed upon an altar, but the predominant offering given upon an altar was a blood offering.

The Hebrew word *mizbeach* is the noun most frequently translated altar. Of the 433 times the word altar is found in the King James Version, 402 times *mizbeach* is the Hebrew word of choice. The purpose for an altar becomes even clearer by looking at the verb form of *mizbeach*, which is *zabach*. *Zabach* literally means to slay, kill, or slaughter for sacrifice. Altars were used primarily as places of sacrifice, especially animal sacrifice. *Mizbeach* corresponds to the Greek word *thusiasterion*, which also refers to the altar for slaying and burning victims or a place of sacrifice.

Why blood? Why would blood be necessary in the worship that man offered to God? Recalling the story of Adam's pre-fall worship, there was no mention of blood. However, God forewarned the first couple that a death penalty would be the result of counterfeit worship. (Gen. 2:17) By honoring the word of the serpent and giving more worth to the creation than to the Creator, Adam failed his worship assignment, committed high treason, and sinned against the commands of God. Adam's penalty was mandated –death!

Shedding of blood fulfills the death sentence. In His providence and wisdom, God instituted a substitutionary system. God would accept the blood of an animal as a temporary payment for the blood of a man. Understanding of this mediatorial system progressively develops throughout the pages of Scripture. In the garden, God took the life of an animal to clothe or cover Adam and Eve. (Gen. 3:21) Their sons, Cain and Abel, brought offerings to God; but God's approval rested upon Abel's blood offering rather than Cain's grain offering. (Gen. 4:3-5) After the flood, Noah's first act upon leaving the ark was to build an altar and offer a blood sacrifice. (Gen. 8:20)

Further clarification of the necessity of blood upon an altar comes as God instructed Moses to establish a sacrificial system for the nation of Israel. Leviticus 17:11 explains how the blood offering would cover the sins of the people. *"For the life of a creature is in the blood, and I have given it to you to make atonement for yourselves on the altar; it is the blood that makes atonement for one's life."* (NIV) Full understanding of God's concealed wisdom found in the substitute's blood and the blood-stained altar would be unveiled in the coming of Jesus and His death at Calvary. (See chapter eight for more details on Christ's blood atonement.)

Once the blood of the substitute is applied to an altar, God can approach man. His justice has been satisfied. Man is free of death's defilement and death's sentence. God does not need to punish; man does not need to fear. God can pronounce a pardon; man can offer his thanksgiving. Man and God are at peace with one another. At blood-stained altars, man and God connect. Altars connect. They connect Heaven and earth, as well as God and man. Altars become an earthly platform from which worship is offered; therefore, from an altar, man can erect a worship canopy or a firmament-tabernacle.

The above referenced passage of Genesis 12 does not tell the exact way Abraham used the altar, but the concept of a blood sacrifice was apparently not uncommon to him as can be seen by his act of killing a ram as a substitute for the sacrifice of his son Isaac. (Gen. 22:13) By whatever means Abraham used the altar at Shechem to offer worship, the point is firmly fixed that he worshipped. Abraham, unlike Adam, passed the worship test on his figurative day two.

Contesting for the Altars

Building altars in an attempt to order man's heaven and thus control the earth is such a powerfully true principle that Satan has long sought to use it for his own perverse purposes. Whoever builds the altars of worship builds the firmament-tabernacle for the god that is being worshipped. Whatever god is enthroned in man's heaven will have a platform for earthly rulership. This was the very attack against Adam's worship in the garden. True worship erects a firmament-tabernacle for God and releases the works of God into the earth. Conversely, false worship sets up a firmament-tabernacle for the devil and releases the works of evil in the earth. Hence, since counterfeit worship is released from counterfeit altars, one might expect a contest over altars.

God is enthroned in the highest Heaven. The Apostle Paul labeled that place of God's Heavenly tabernacle as the third Heaven. (II. Cor. 12:2) Satan, who formerly was an archangel, attempted to erect another worship canopy in God's highest Heaven, which was directed at himself rather than at God. He enlisted a third of the heavenly host in his counterfeit worship; and for this, he and his followers were expelled from God's tabernacle-throne. (Is. 14:12-15; Ez. 28:12-19) The third Heaven with its tabernacle was reserved only for the worship of God.

As has already been discussed, man was to order his heaven after the pattern in the highest Heaven by erecting a worship firmament for God in man's sphere. Bible expositors often refer to man's heaven as the second heaven. (The atmospheric heaven constitutes the first heaven.) Falling for the serpent's enticement, Adam and Eve worshipped a false god, set up a counterfeit tabernacle, and enthroned demonic spirits upon their praises. Thus, the location of devilish influence became entrenched in the second heaven. (Eph. 3:10; 6:12; Col. 2:15)

Since Eden, the primary contest has been for control of man's heaven. Demonically-inspired altars offer worship to appease, empower, and release the influence of Satan and his fallen angelic host from the second heaven. God-inspired altars offer worship to extol, honor, and release the influence of God and His holy angelic host from the third Heaven. The more effective the God-inspired altars, the less effective the demonically-inspired altars and vice versa.

The concept of constructing altars to open and release the spiritual realm into man's spheres of activities is much the emphasis of ancient pagan religions, the occult, and new age practices. Words used to describe the heavenly openings created at altars include ziggurats, vortex, axis mundi, and portals. Ziggurats began to be constructed around 2200 BC and were common to Sumerians, Babylonians and Assyrians of ancient Mesopotamia. Today, the remnants of about 25 remain. Constructed like an Egyptian pyramid, the square mountains of stone were temple towers built to be a bridge between heaven and earth. The Sumerian ziggurat known as Etemenanki, meaning house or foundation of heaven on earth, was believed to be a vertical bond between heaven and earth.

Axis mundi means world axis or axis of the world. The axis mundi is believed to connect heaven and earth as well as to provide a path between the two. Many cultures consider a specific place, almost always a hill, a mountain, or a pyramid to be the axis mundi. For the Sioux, the Black Hills was the axis mundi; while Mount Kailash is holy to several religions in Tibet. The Dome of the Rock for Islam is considered to be the place where Muhammed was raised and lowered from heaven. The ancient Greeks had several sites that were considered places of connection, sometimes called omphalos or navel stone. Other religions build structures to be metaphoric or representative axis mundi: totem poles, ziggurats, or the minaret of a mosque.

The new age movement combines scientific investigation with ancient mysticism. The location of power fields or magnetic fields on the earth are considered to be the geographical connection points to the spirit world. The intersection of heaven and earth is called either a vortex or a portal.

The occult has historically practiced setting up altars for the purpose of opening a portal to release demonic beings. All counterfeit altars to open heaven stand in opposition and are an antithesis to God's will. They function to empower the devil or his demons, because altars serve as gateways to control heavenly traffic. Conversely, true God-ordained altars function to connect Heaven and earth.

Locating the Altars

Because altars function as gateways, it comes as no surprise to find altars erected at gates, doors, and points of entry. An illustration can be drawn from everyday life. A road or a path links points of exit and entry to one another. Traveling from one destination to another is accomplished by exiting through one gate, i.e. a front door, the city limits, or the border of a nation, and traveling along some form of a pathway until one arrives at the gate of the destination, i.e. another front door, a different city limits, or the border of another nation. The example of this common practice provides an explanation of a spiritual pattern. Altars open gates or doors that allow traffic between the spiritual and the physical realm to move along a pathway or through a portal. An important principle emerges: he who controls the gates by way of the altars controls the traffic between the dimensions.

Several biblical passages confirm that God set great importance on locating altars at doors. Moses was instructed by God to build a house or to pitch a tent in which God would reside. God gave the pattern for the Tabernacle, and Moses was strictly warned to build it exactly after the blueprint that God had given. (Ex. 25:40; Heb. 8:5) A brazen altar upon which sacrifices were offered was positioned at the opening or entrance of the Tabernacle. The Tabernacle was so constructed that man entered at the east and God resided at the opposite end on the west. The altar acted as a door, which opened a pathway between the dimension of man and the dimension of God.

During the days of Josiah, King of Judah, shrines or altars dedicated to other gods stood at the gate to the city of the governor. (II Kin. 23:5-8) Josiah tore down the altars. His actions were equivalent to shutting the earthly gate to a demonic portal. With the altar gone and the gate closed, devils could not traffic from the second heaven to the earth.

A third illustration is found in the law of Moses. If a man or woman in Israel was found guilty of idol worship, that person was to be taken to the city gates and stoned to death. (Deut. 17:2-8) Why at the gates? All persons entering into or exiting from a city would have to do so by the gate. The elders of the city were responsible to guard the gate and insure that only law-abiding people entered. Those persons who kill, steal, and destroy were not to be given entrance. They also set the judgment seats at the city's gates, thus declaring that only just judgments would be allowed inside of the city. An idolater's counterfeit altar opened a gate to spiritual traffic. The idolaters' gate was not to be approved by the elders. Those spirits that kill, steal, and destroy were not to be given entrance. Therefore, in the one act of executing the death penalty at the city's gates, it closed the spiritual gate and it testified that the righteous stood guard over all gates, thus all traffic, into their city. The stoning at the gate was equivalent to destroying the altar, closing the demonic portal, and reclaiming the city's gate for God.

Altars were also erected at high places, like the tops of mountains either natural or man-made. Using high places was a symbolic claim to the right to ascend as near to Heaven as possible and, from that vantagepoint, to have the power to open a Heavenly gate. Erecting altars in high places for the purpose of idol worship was strictly forbidden in Scripture and was often the cause of God's disciplinary judgments against Israel. (II Kin. 17:9-12)

Raising Altars: The Abrahamic Strategy

In Abraham's day, the practice of erecting altars at gates or in high places was well established as part of heathenistic worship. However, God had promised to give to Abraham and to his heirs the land that was occupied by idolaters and controlled by the demonic spirits. God gave Abraham the strategy. Abraham traveled throughout the land raising altars to the Living God.

Genesis 12:6-8; 13:18; 22:9: *"And Abram passed through the land unto the place of Sichem, unto the plain of Moreh. And the Canaanite was then in the land. And the Lord appeared unto Abram, and said, Unto thy seed will I give this land: and there builded he an altar unto the Lord, who appeared unto him. And he removed from thence unto a mountain on the east of Bethel, and pitched his tent, having Bethel on the west, and Hai on the east: and there he builded an altar unto the Lord, and called upon the name of the Lord. . . . Then Abram removed his tent, and came and dwelt in the plain of Mamre, which is in Hebron, and built there an altar unto the Lord. . . . And they came to the place which God had told him of; and Abraham built an altar there, and laid the wood in order, and bound Isaac his son, and laid him on the altar upon the wood."*

When Abraham arrived in his promised land, he built an altar at Shechem and called upon the name of the Lord.   This deed was more than act of piety, beyond humble acknowledgement of God's providence, and even went further than offering thanks for God's promises. He staked a claim for God. He opened an earthly gate for Heavenly traffic in the midst of a demon-controlled land. He was contending with demonic gods worshipped by the Canaanites and with the activities of a godless people who ruled the land, as exemplified by the citizens of Sodom and Gomorrah.

From Shechem, Abraham moved to Bethel where he erected a second altar. (Gen. 12:7) Famine drove him to Egypt; but when he returned to Canaan, he came again to Bethel and the altar. (Gen. 13:3-4) *"There Abram called on the name of the LORD."* There was no need for Abraham to call on the name of the Lord from the altar if he did not understand that the altar provided a meeting place. He had gone to Egypt where, after a threatening situation with Pharaoh, Abraham had been sent out of Egypt with all his possessions. He returned to a land that had been promised to him but was still occupied by idol worshippers. He returned to Bethel. Possibly, he decided upon the area because he was already familiar with the territory having dwelled there previously. Possibly, he decided to return to the area because it was bountiful and his herds and flocks were abundant. Although these reasons may all be true, the greater reason he returned is defined in the passage. He returned to the altar at Bethel.

Abraham connected with the gate to Heaven. He believed Bethel was a gateway, because he called upon God from there. He could have called upon God during his journey from Egypt to Canaan. No doubt he did. He could have prayed in his tent, in the desert, on a mountain, in an oasis. No doubt he did. But at Bethel he reestablished the earthly gate for Heavenly traffic in the midst of that demon-controlled land. It was a good thing that he did. Within a short time he was forced to go to war against four mighty kings with just his household servants. (Gen. 14) Scripture calls it a slaughter. Abraham's altar opened Heaven's traffic, and Abraham prevailed.

Another move took him to Hebron where again he built an altar unto the Lord. (Gen. 13:18) At the command for Abraham to sacrifice Isaac, the patriarch erected yet one more altar. (Gen. 22) This time he built on Mt. Moriah. Abraham built altars. Each time he did, he offered worship. All the acts of worship were not just an end unto themselves. They were part of a greater spiritual plan for reconstruction. God wanted worship that could reorder the heaven. A reconstructed heaven will create an atmosphere whereby the earth can respond. God promised Abraham that his altars, especially the one on which he was willing to offer Isaac, would profoundly change man's heaven and the earth.

Genesis 22:16-18: *"And said, By myself have I sworn, saith the Lord, for because thou hast done this thing, and hast not withheld thy son, thine only son: That in blessing I will bless thee, and in multiplying I will multiply thy seed as the stars of the heaven, and as the sand which is upon the sea shore; and thy seed shall possess the gate of his*

enemies; And in thy seed shall all the nations of the earth
be blessed; because thou hast obeyed my voice."

By a life of building worship altars, which culminated with the final act of offering his most treasured possession, Abraham proved that he honored, esteemed, and valued God above all else. If, in reality, those acts of worship had the ability to erect a God-ordained firmament in man's heaven, then there should be some indication of a change in the order of heaven. Indeed there was. God spoke. He told Abraham to look to the heaven and see the stars, which represented the seed of righteous Abraham. Certainly God was saying that Abraham's lineage would be vast. But, the metaphor of choice was concerning the arrangement of the skies.

In Eden, the serpent gained access to the gate of heaven. Adam empowered the enemy. Adam opened man's heaven to the serpent affording him authority to rule from the counterfeit tabernacle that was erected by Adam's false worship. One could say that Adam's deeds made room for false stars. When making the promise to Abraham, God was forecasting a change in the heaven.

The serpent also gained access to gates in the earth through Adam's sin. Earth felt the sway. Illegitimate rulers with ungodly actions brought the world to the edge of destruction, namely Noah's flood. But Abraham had been building a new firmament-tabernacle, and God was likewise forecasting a corresponding change in the earth. God spoke. The seed of righteous Abraham would be so abundant on the earth that it could only be compared to the sand of the seas.

Contained within this same blessing to Abraham was a promise that he would possess the gate of his enemies. Enemies in the gates of man's counterfeit heaven and enemies in the gates of man's counterfeit earthly systems would become subject to this new 'adam' who worshipped. The Abrahamic strategy of raising altars would transform the heaven and transfigure the earth.

CHAPTER THREE

Jacob: The Experience of Finding the Portal

Passing on the Pattern

The promises that God made to Abraham were not only for him but were also for his heirs. He would be the father of many nations. (Gen. 17:4-5) In him all the nations of the earth would be blessed. (Gen. 18:18) His seed would possess the gates of his enemies. (Gen. 22:17) Amazing promises! Incredible pledges! Unimaginable possibilities! What was Abraham's response to these tremendous and far-reaching Words? The Bible says that he believed; Abraham was a man of faith. (Rom. 4:11-13; Gal. 3:7-9; Heb. 11:8-19)

His belief that God was both willing and able to perform the promises prompted Abraham to act. He moved from his homeland. He built altars and cut covenant with God. He was so thoroughly persuaded that his son Isaac was his promised heir that he feared not to offer him as a sacrifice. Indeed, Abraham's faith was affirmed by his actions, declared by his deeds, certified by his conduct.

The promises, which God gave to Abraham, extended to his son and his heirs for many generations. Therefore, one of the most outstanding works done by this father was to train his progeny in faith and obedience. God knew His servant Abraham. *"For I know him, that he will command his children and his household after him, and they shall keep the way of the Lord, to do justice and judgment; that the Lord may bring upon Abraham that which he hath spoken of him."* (Gen. 18:19) Abraham taught his children to build altars.

Genesis 26:23-25: *"And he (Isaac) went up from thence to Beer-sheba. And the Lord appeared unto him the same night, and said, I am the God of Abraham thy father: fear not, for I am with thee, and will bless thee, and multiply thy seed for my servant Abraham's sake. And he builded an altar there, and called upon the name of the Lord and pitched his tent there: and there Isaac's servants digged a well."*

The re-creation pattern already applied to the life of Adam and of Abraham can again be discovered in Isaac. God appeared to him during the nighttime breaking through the darkness with His Word and called him into the Abrahamic covenant. God spoke and the light dawned. That was his day one. His response was the same as his father's; he built an altar. That was his day two. Isaac established an altar of worship, thereby erecting his firmament-tabernacle. Like his father, Abraham, he dedicated his heaven to the Almighty, claimed the right to open a portal for God, and continued to sustain claim over the land from the god of the Canaanites. Isaac contended with the demon gods by building an altar to consecrate the firmament and release Heaven into the earth.

Abraham's grandson, Jacob, also practiced building altars. Upon arriving in Shechem, which was the first city in which Grandfather Abraham had erected an altar, Jacob bought a piece of land, pitched his tent upon the land, and set up an altar at the site. *"And he erected there an altar, and called it El-elohe-Israel."* (Gen. 33:20) What an amazing announcement he made! El-elohe-Israel – the mighty God of Israel! He was not proclaiming that God was the mighty God over the yet-to-be-formed nation of Israel; he was proclaiming that God was the mighty God over himself, Jacob, whose name had recently been changed from Jacob to Israel.

Again the pattern of re-creation is evident. God separated Jacob's metaphoric darkness by introducing the light of a name change from Jacob, which means the deceiver, to Israel, which means the prince of God. His name change was representative of a change in his nature. Jacob experienced a day one. What did Jacob do on his metaphoric day two? Jacob worshipped. He built an altar, claimed the heaven for El-elohe-Israel, and pitched a firmament-tabernacle.

Meeting God Under an Open Heaven

The altar at Shechem was not Jacob's first encounter with an altar. Jacob was the second born twin of Isaac and Rebekah. God had announced to Rebekah that her older child would serve the younger. (Gen. 25:23) Jacob must have grown up with his mother recounting the Words of God to him; because he sought several opportunities to position himself for the elder son privileges, which was a double-portion of the inheritance and the rights to manage the family's assets. As Isaac neared death, he began the process of ordering his affairs and appointing his heir. Jacob and his mother devised a scheme to deceive the nearly-blind father into thinking Jacob was the elder brother in order that Isaac would mistakenly bless Jacob. The plan succeeded. Jacob received the birthright blessing, which was the promise made to Abraham.

Upon gaining the knowledge that he had been cheated, the eldest son set his heart to kill Jacob. To preserve their son's life, Jacob's parents sent him to the home of Rebekah's brother. In flight as a refugee, Jacob encountered God.

Genesis 28:10-13, 16-19: *"And Jacob went out from Beer-sheba, and went toward Haran. And he lighted upon a certain place, and tarried there all night, because the sun was set; and he took of the stones of that place, and put them for his pillows, and lay down in that place to sleep. And he dreamed, and behold a ladder set up on the earth, and the top of it reached to heaven: and behold the angels of God ascending and descending on it. And, behold, the Lord stood above it, and said, I am the Lord God of Abraham thy father, and the God of Isaac: the land whereon thou liest, to thee will I give it, and to thy seed; . . . . And Jacob awaked out of his sleep, and he said, Surely the Lord is in this place; and I knew it not. And he was afraid, and said, How dreadful is this place! This is none other but the house of God, and this is the gate of heaven. And Jacob rose up early in the morning, and took the stone that he had put for his pillows, and set it up for a pillar, and poured oil upon the top of it. And he called the name of that place Bethel: but the name of that city was called Luz at the first."*

Jacob encountered God at Bethel. He experienced a ladder that reached from Heaven to the earth. He saw angels descending from Heaven to earth and ascending back again to Heaven. God stood above the ladder and Jacob resided on the earth at the base of the stairway. He found a pathway between the two realms, became aware of a place where the two dimensions connected, and discovered a spot where a gate to Heavenly traffic had been opened. Jacob located a portal. What gave rise to such a place? How, when, and where did Bethel become a gate to Heaven?

Genesis 12:8 records that Abraham built his second altar at Bethel. Over 100 years before Jacob laid his head on a rock to sleep under nature's open heaven, his grandfather had erected a firmament-tabernacle through his altar building and thus created a spiritual open Heaven. There, Jacob met God.

The Bible opens with a portrait of Adam and mankind, representatively, living under an open Heaven in the Garden of Eden. The Bible closes with a similar description of redeemed mankind again dwelling with God without separation, division, or barrier in the New Jerusalem. (Rev. 22:2-3) If Scripture begins with an open Heaven and ends with an open Heaven, then it is reasonable to conclude that God's will is for earth to be under an open Heaven. As this is undoubtedly the purpose of God, it is likewise reasonable to deduce that other places can be found in Scripture where Heaven-earth connections occur. Jacob's Bethel is just one of many of those places. Jacob's Bethel is a retro look at Adam's heaven and a forward look at the heavens yet to be established. (More on Jacob's ladder will be discussed in chapter eight.)

Jacob responded by declaring, *"The Lord is in this place, and I knew it not."* (Gen. 28:16) When the light of the portal broke in on him, Jacob went to worship. He set up a stone altar. He called on the name of God. He vowed a vow of consecration. All these deeds were acts of worship. Jacob enacted the Abrahamic covenant by offering the tithe even as his grandfather had done. (Gen. 28:22; Gen. 14:20) The altar built by the worship of Abraham was being maintained by the worship of Jacob. The portal opened by the grandfather was being preserved by the grandson.

Jacob declared an amazing revelation. He called the name of the place Bethel, which means the house of God. He recognized that mankind could find a portal when mankind found God's house on the earth. The purpose of every Bethel, therefore, is to be a gate to heaven.

Contending with Counterfeit Gates to Heaven

The most famous counterfeit 'bethel' is the Tower of Babel. (Gen. 11:1-9) What was the nature of this tower? Why did the builders want a structure whose top would reach to heaven? From where did the evil thoughts and imaginations arise that prompted the builders to erect the tower? To understand the nature and purpose of this tower, a reflective review of the effects of sin before and after the flood of Noah's day is necessary.

The sin of Adam did not take long to express itself in the actions of one man to his neighbor. The son of Adam, Cain, killed his brother Abel. Murder, false dominion, ungodly rulership, and self-promoting power were the preferred man-to-man relational lifestyle that resulted from sin. The seventh generation from Cain produced a man named Lamech, whose murderous deeds caused the testimony, *"If Cain shall be avenged sevenfold, truly Lamech seventy and sevenfold."* (Gen. 4:24)

Before his death, Abel had responded to God by building an altar and offering a blood sacrifice. As has already been discussed, an altar dedicated to God has the effect of opening the Heaven. God gave to Adam and Eve a replacement son for the murdered Abel, who was named Seth. Seth represented the righteous lineage of Abel. The seventh generation from Seth produced a man named Enoch, who walked with God under an open Heaven. (Heb. 11:5)

During the days of Enoch and his sons, the world became increasingly wicked. Genesis 6:5 declares, *"And*

God saw that the wickedness of man was great in the earth, and that every imagination of the thoughts of his heart was only evil continually." Several conditions can be sighted for the increase in wickedness. The first was the presence of giants or Nephilim, which are beings that resulted from the union of the Sons of God and the daughters of men. (Gen. 6:4) This passage has three traditional interpretations. Some expositors have taught that the "Sons of God" were fallen angels whose transgression of sexual sin with women produced the race of giants and resulted in those sinning angels being bound and cast into torment awaiting the final judgment. This interpretation is supported by the Book of Enoch, which is non-canonical literature. A portion of the prophecy of Enoch, however, is recorded in Jude 1:14. (Enoch 1:9) Enoch himself is identified for his life of faith (Heb. 11:5) and for his placement in the genealogy of Christ. (Lk. 3:24-38) Therefore, many theologians place a limited measure of credibility, although not divine inspiration, upon the Book of Enoch.

The second proposed origin of the Nephilim postulates that the descendants of the righteous lineage of Seth ("the Sons of God") intermarried with Cain's evil descendants ("the daughters of men"), thus weakening the good influence of the faithful and resulting in increased moral depravity in the world. The third accepted interpretation postulates that powerful princes married and produced children that were almost limitless in their exercise of force over the earth's population. Whatever the origin of the race of Nephilim, sin proliferated to such elevated levels of immorality and violence that God pronounced judgment upon the whole earth.

A second reason for the increased wickedness can be found through application of already known principles. Adam enthroned the devil and his fallen angelic hosts. From the realms of the second heaven, satanic powers influenced human activity. Paul taught the Ephesian church that their pre-Christian behavior was driven by the high-ranking devilish rulers whose influence was expressed in human actions. (Eph. 2:1-3) A cycle was created. Earthly altars dedicated to the devil create a demonically-infested heaven that yielded a demonically-influenced earth. From the demonically-influenced earth, men built yet more altars through which a demonically-infested heaven was fortified and by which counterfeit portals were opened to release evil powers upon mankind. Such was the condition pre-flood.

The Book of Enoch speaks of fallen angels teaching men how to practice charms, enchantments, and other occult activities. Although the writings of Enoch cannot be used to positively prove the source of man's knowledge of these practices, the first three chapters of Genesis definitively depict the serpent as teaching Adam and Eve how to enthrone the Devil in man's heaven. If pre-fall man was prompted by the chief fallen angel to create a throne for Satan, certainly post-fall man could be taught by fallen angels to open portals to release satanic power. The knowledge that these crafts exist, if not the origin of the knowledge, is taught in the pages of Scripture; and covenant men are repeatedly warned not to practice any sorcery, divination, incantations, or other black arts. However pre-diluvian man learned the counterfeit worship practices, they abounded. The demonically-structured heaven released such a demonically-structured earth that *"it was corrupt and the earth was filled with violence."* (Gen. 6:11)

God brought a flood over the whole earth that destroyed all living creatures except for Enoch's great-grandson Noah, his three sons and their wives, and the animals sheltered in the ark. When at last the waters receded and the door of the ark could be opened, the light of a new day dawned upon Noah. What was his re-creative response? He worshipped. *"And Noah builded an altar unto the Lord; and took of every clean beast, and of every clean fowl, and offered burnt offerings on the altar. And the Lord smelled a sweet savour."* (Gen. 8:20-21a)

God had restructured the heaven with the rains and a rainbow and reordered the earth through the upheaval of the flood. Noah, another replacement 'adam', was granted dominion over the new creation. (Gen. 9:1-17) Noah's altar-building activity was a godly response; it was day-two, firmament-tabernacle worship. Noah was staking a claim in man's heaven for the glory of God to be released.

Noah's sons were Shem, Ham, and Japheth. This scripture tells of Ham who entered into his father's tent at a time when Noah was drunk from wine. Ham took advantage of his sleeping father and *"saw the nakedness of his father, and told his two brethren without."* (Gen. 9:22) Although the exact meaning of "saw the nakedness" is obscure, the context indicates that the deed was beyond an accidental observation. Leviticus 18:7-20 uses the same phraseology in the context of sexual prohibitions. The law stated that no one could have sexual relationship, which was termed uncovering the nakedness, with any family member listed in the passage. Ham's action against his father seemed of the same nature as that which was forbidden. There is an indication that Ham's seeing was accompanied by an act that was probably sexual, because Noah awoke and recognized what his son had done unto him. (Gen. 9:24)

Although the passage remains somewhat undefined as to the exact deed, certainly Ham demonstrated a lack of respect and a mocking attitude for his father's sexuality. The level of the transgression caused Noah to place a curse upon Ham and his heirs. Ham's action was an indication that the pre-flood attitude toward sexual corruption and ungodly treatment of one's fellowman had permeated Ham and had been carried over into the new day.

The Bible indicates that Ham not only retained and practiced some pre-fall abominations but that he passed that knowledge down to his heirs. It is easy to imagine that those possessing information of the former world order would have had many opportunities to share the stories. Only a verbal record remained, and Noah and his family were the scroll upon which all pre-flood knowledge was written. Descriptions of the landscape before the flood had altered its appearance must have aroused the interests of the children born post-flood. Explanations of the civilizations, the inventions, the technical advancements, or the industrial capabilities must have provided interesting narratives. Giants with big swords slaying fire-breathing dragons may have been more fact than fiction. And what was told of the giants? Bedtime sagas of their might and bravery that caused them to be unstoppable could have stirred the envy of every young boy. If the pre-flood chronicles were recounted outside of the context of sin, of righteous judgment, or God's prevailing wisdom, then the hearers might have longed to regain the good old days. Tracing the lineage of Ham validates that ungodly practices were passed through family lines.

The third generation from cursed Ham was a man named Nimrod, whose name means rebel. Scripture declared him to be a mighty hunter, a description that revealed his prowess, courage, leadership, and fearlessness. Whether he was a champion hunter of wild game or a conquering warrior over people groups is not fully disclosed. However, he took lands and built cities. In the spirit of the pre-flood giants, Nimrod became a mighty man of renown who used his dominion over others and his oppressive tactics to form a kingdom for himself. Of the many cities under his government, Babel is named. (Gen. 10:8-12; 11:1-9)

Babel, which was later called Babylon, was more than a city. Genesis 11:4 says that both a city and a tower were constructed. The purpose of the city is defined by the name. Babel means the gate of god. Historical records describe the building of a ziggurat dedicated to a god named Marduk, which was Babylon's chief deity. Written accounts say that this tower temple was created by the same process defined in the Genesis 11 passage and that every brick was inscribed with the name of Marduk. Whether or not the preserved history is describing the same Tower of Babel in the Bible, certainly the style of building and the purpose for building Babylonian towers are verified. Nimrod built an altar to demonic powers.

In the same spirit of pre-flood rebellion, occult practices and portal-opening activities had been re-engaged. The builders wanted a tower whose base would be on the earth but whose top would reach into the heaven. (Gen. 11:4) The parallel to Jacob's ladder is unmistakable.

Nimrod and his associates wanted to create a ladder to heaven and a highway for the traffic of the satanic powers. The Tower of Babel was erected to establish a devilish firmament-tabernacle.

As has been established, the way man structures his heaven will determine the blessing or the curse that results in the earth. The idea of a demonically-infested Babylonian heaven yielding a demonically-influenced Babylonian earth is developed within the pages of Scripture. The term Babylon becomes a generic label for any idolatrous city under the influence of the Devil rather than always referring to a geographical location on the earth. In this context, Babylon is called a dwelling place of dragons (Jer. 51:47), the mother of all covenant-breaking idolatry (Rev. 17:5), and a habitation of devils and every foul spirit. (Rev. 18:2) Nimrod set about to league with satanic powers to aid him in his quest for domination.

The Bible also traces the godly line of Shem. Shem would have known the ways of Enoch. Shem watched his father, Noah, build an altar upon exiting the ark. The godly line of Shem contested with the ungodly line of Ham for control of the altars, thus for control of the heavenly portals. Each line had knowledge that altars open gates to an invisible, unseen realm. Shem's ancestor Jacob discovered that the gate to Heaven could be found at an earthly house of God or a Bethel.

Building Bethel

Various houses of God are described within the pages of Scripture. In each tabernacle, each Bethel, a portal to the third Heaven is opened through which man and God can connect. Abraham, Isaac, and Jacob erected altars in the open air. No formal mention of a house for God occurred until the time of Moses, when God called for the altar to be set inside of a tent. The truths established in the open-air altars continued to exist while more revelation of God's purpose was added under the next phase of indoor-altars.

Similar Bethels are found in the Tabernacle of David and the Temple of Solomon. God continued to unfold Kingdom purpose and meaning through each successive house of God; but the knowledge that each Bethel was a portal remained consistent from tent to temple, from Old Covenant to New Covenant, from the house that Moses built to the house that Jesus built.

CHAPTER FOUR

Moses: The Call to Build God's House

Tracing the Lineage

The sons of Noah multiplied in the earth. Ham's lineage not only produced Cush, the father of Babel's infamous Nimrod, but he also fathered Mizraim, Phut, and Canaan.   As already noted, Nimrod is credited with occupying Babylon and Assyria. (Mic. 5:6)   However, other Cushites settled south of Egypt in an area called Ethiopia (not to be confused with the modern nation of the same name). Egypt is called in Scripture the land of Ham. (Ps. 105:23; 106:22) Phut's progeny settled in a region of Africa bordering Egypt generally identified as Libya, and the men of Phut (Put) were renowned as mercenaries or soldiers for hire.   Mizraim's children took residence throughout Egypt, a civilization known for pyramid ziggurats and the worship of other gods. Finally, Canaan's descendants occupied the territory called by the same name, Canaan, and the inhabitants became so vile and idolatrous that God promised to displace them and give the land to Abraham. The warrior spirit and the occult practices of pre-flood giants prevailed in all the sons of Ham.

The generations of Shem, Noah's righteous son, can be traced to the twelve sons of Jacob, which eventually developed into the nation of Israel. The Scripture records the story of a sibling rivalry and jealousy between Jacob's twelve sons that resulted in the eleventh-born son, Joseph, being sold into Midianite and then Egyptian slavery. By the sovereign hand of God, Joseph was eventually promoted to assist the Pharaoh, Egypt's king, in a massive food stockpiling program in preparation of a seven-year famine that God had warned was coming. As the famine spread throughout the surrounding nations, Jacob, his eleven other sons, and their families were affected. Upon traveling to Egypt to buy grain, the brothers were reunited with Joseph. From his high-ranking position, Joseph made provision for the whole budding nation of Israel to migrate and colonize in Egypt.

After the death of Joseph and the monarch that he served, other Pharaohs arose that did not remember Joseph. Israel lost favor and became slaves to the Egyptians. An edict went forth to kill all the boy babies of the Israelites in an attempt to limit the population that might grow and seek to overthrow the tyrannical rulers. During this period of biblical history, an Israelite child named Moses was born. In fear of the child's death, Moses' mother hid the baby in a basket near the river's edge where the daughter of Pharaoh found him. Moses, the son of Levi, the son of Jacob, who descended from Abraham, who descended from Shem, was raised as a son of Pharaoh. In due time, Moses sought to help his own by taking vengeance upon a cruel Egyptian taskmaster. When news returned to Pharaoh that Moses had killed the Egyptian, Moses fled to Midian for his life.

Moses took residence in the home of Jethro, married, fathered two sons, and took up the trade of a shepherd until one day:

Exodus 3:1-2, 7, 10-12:   " Now Moses kept the flock of Jethro his father in law, the priest of Midian: and he led the flock to the backside of the desert, and came to the mountain of God, even to Horeb. And the angel of the Lord appeared unto him in a flame of fire out of the midst of a bush: and he looked, and, behold, the bush burned with fire, and the bush was not consumed. . . . And the Lord said, I have surely seen the affliction of my people which are in Egypt, and have heard their cry by reason of their taskmasters; for I know their sorrows; . . . Come now therefore, and I will send thee unto Pharaoh, that thou mayest bring forth my people the children of Israel out of Egypt. And Moses said unto God, Who am I, that I should go unto Pharaoh, and that I should bring forth the children of Israel out of Egypt? And he said, Certainly I will be with thee; and this shall be a token unto thee, that I have sent thee: When thou hast brought forth the people out of Egypt, ye shall serve God upon this mountain. "

Egypt, the seed of Ham, was oppressing Israel, the seed of Shem. Light dawned from a bush that burned but was not consumed by the fire. God's Word broke through the darkness. A new day one was dawning upon Moses and upon Israel. They were both being called into day-two worship. Eventually, they would be positioned to build a new earth, fulfilling the three-day, re-creation pattern.

Meeting God at a Burning Bush

A Heavenly visitor encircled in light and non-consuming fire describes properties contained in a portal. Moses' burning bush was, indeed, a portal. It manifested the aspects of glory consistent with the experiences of Abraham and Jacob, and it transported a Heavenly being. To further verify that it was an opening into Heaven, the voice of God spoke from the midst of the glory shaft. The imagery is consistent with phenomena found in Jacob's ladder.

God identified Himself with the children of Shem by declaring *"I am the God of thy father, the God of Abraham, the God of Isaac, and the God of Jacob."* (Ex. 3:6) The portals created in former generations had opened over Moses. He was being called, like his predecessors, to structure his heaven so that he could release Heaven into the earth. He was being commissioned to challenge the ancestors of Ham, the Egyptians, which would mean engaging spirits liken unto those of the pre-flood giants and contesting for dominion over heaven. He was being asked to go head to head with the chief deity of Egypt, Pharaoh.

Concerned that no one would believe him, Moses requested a symbol of validation. God pointed out the shepherd's rod that was in Moses' hand. A rod is an extension of the hand, therefore representative of the tool or the trade. Modern day examples of this principle still exist: the scepter of a king, the baton of an orchestra conductor, or the staff of a military field marshal. Moses was a shepherd and his rod not only aided him in his duties but identified his role.

His role was about to change. His new title would be that of a prophet-deliverer. He would hear from Heaven, speak for God, overthrow the evil rulers, and bring God's people out from under the demonic heaven of Egypt. He needed a symbol of his new calling. God told him to cast the shepherd's rod to the ground. It became a serpent. God instructed Moses to pick the snake up by the tail; and when he did, it straightened out and became a rod again. His reconstructed rod conveyed, among other things, that he would have power to 'straighten out' the works of the serpent. He was granted authority to defeat all devils that oppressively ruled God's elect.

The rod was more than a symbol. It became a power tool used in the working of signs and miracles. (Ex. 4:17) Egypt had its own source of power wands, the rods of the sorcerers. Upon the first contest with Pharaoh, Moses cast down his rod, which turned into a serpent as it had at the burning bush. Unimpressed by the miracle, the magicians likewise turned their poles into serpents through enchantments. The first miracle in Egypt was a contest to reveal the spiritual power level of the men who used the rods. Whereas God's man had a rod that channeled power from the spiritual dimension of God's Heaven, the devil's men had magic wands that channeled power from the spiritual dimension of the second heaven. God proved his superior abilities. The serpent-rod of Moses swallowed up the serpent-rods of the sorcerers. (Ex. 7:10-13)

Throughout the annals of time, contained within the fairytales of children, and recorded in 'how to' manuals of the black arts, the magic wand is the occult practitioner's tool. A magic wand is used to throw spells, conjure apparitions, cast circles, or do whatever the sorcerer wants. It is seen as a conduit or conductor to open doorways into different dimensions and direct spiritual forces. Although they differ in styles, shapes, and materials used for construction, all wands serve the purpose of empowering the owner with supernatural abilities. The form and the materials of the wand are usually chosen to match the use. Built into the wand are correspondences, which are symbols or items from the material world that have a non-material counterpart in the spirit world. The idea is to affect the one realm by manipulation of the corresponding item in the other realm, similar to that which occurs in voodoo when pins are placed in a doll that represents the person upon whom the magician wishes to bring pain.

Wands can also contain empowerment options, like the insertion of sacred artifacts into the shaft such as soil from a particular holy site or an object with special occult meaning. The small insertion functions as a bridge between the earthly, sorcerer's realm and intangible, demonic world. Once created, the wand is consecrated or 'enlivened' by a particular ceremony or incantation. The consecrated wand acts like a mystical axis between the two realms. It could be likened to a transportable portal used to release the demonic kingdom into the realms of man.

Moses departed the burning bush with a consecrated rod. Moses' rod conveyed the office into which he had been sovereignly called and the holy ground upon which his rod had been hallowed. It was not magical. God would not respond to human manipulations or rituals. Moses walked in ethics and lived by faith, which was the reason his rod had power. Conversely, occult rods communicate leagues made with the devil through ritualistic vows and covenants. They are signposts that the devil has granted some otherworldly power to the user who serves the forces of darkness. Satanic followers walk in evil ways and live controlled by fear.

Moses engaged the sorcerers of Egypt who had magic wands empowered by the demon gods of the land. Two representative agents of two diversely opposing kingdoms contested over the control of heaven. The satanic priests were schooled in the black arts, opened portals to devils, and performed supernatural deeds by demonic powers. Moses was called as a prophet-deliverer and given a rod to serve as a conduit for the supernatural power of God. The rod of Moses prevailed over the magic wands of witchcraft. After the ten plagues, which were really heaven-releasing, portal-opening miracles, Pharaoh set the nation of Israel free.

Dwelling Under an Open Heaven

The exact pathway for the Exodus of the nation of Israel was clearly mapped; because the Lord went before them in a glory-cloud, fire-filled pillar. (Ex. 13:21) The pillar had its base in the earth, its top in the Heaven, and a pathway between the two realms. The connection with Jacob's ladder is again unmistakable. The nation moved out of Egypt under a portal. The Egyptian heaven had been reordered by God's judgments. Moses had broken open the demonic heaven. He had destroyed the second heaven power base of satanic control. The highest Heaven rushed in. Glory broke through. God's portal was opened over the nation of Israel.

Earlier references to portals had identified various phenomenon of Heaven, like light, fire, and God's voice that were made manifest when a connection between the two realms occurred. In the Exodus portal, a new observable fact can be found. The portal was described as a cloud. The Hebrew word translated cloud in Exodus 13:21 is *'anan*. The first usage of *'anan* is found after Noah's flood when God set a rainbow in the cloud. Both the cloud and the bow were marking God's covenant promise. He was making a proclamation to the earth from man's heaven that had been reordered by His judgment. The second use of *'anan* is in the cloud pillar found at the Exodus. Again, God was marking a covenant promise. Again, God was testifying to the earth from man's heaven that had been reordered by His judgment. God appeared. His glory was seen in the cloud.

The King James Version translates *'anan* as cloud 58 times in the Scriptures. With few exceptions, the Bible is not speaking of the condensation of vapors in rain clouds as a feature of weather but rather uses the term cloud when there is a manifestation of God's presence, either in His goodness or His severity. (Understanding the cloud-like nature of the glory will expand the comprehension of portal theology and shall be discussed in more detail in chapter five.)

The pillar was described as a cloud by day and as fire by night that went before the nation to guide them as they journeyed. During daylight hours, the fire within was less visible because of the brightness of the sun. Therefore, the pillar was described as a cloud. During the hours of darkness, the fire within radiated out to light the way. At that time, the pillar was described as a fire. The fire or light, however, was ever present in the pillar. When the glory cloud appeared over the Israelites, a light source became available in man's heaven that did not originate from the sun, moon, or stars. The light came from God and was a manifestation of God. This is reminiscent of God's creation pattern. On day one, God sent a Heaven-originated light source to illuminate the earth that He was forming.

Earlier patriarchs had been replacement 'adams' and had been offered the opportunity to follow God's three-day creation pattern. As has already been discussed, the righteous seed line worshipped on the figurative day two as a response to light dawning on the figurative day one. At this point in biblical history, rather than an individual man replacing 'adam,' God was calling a nation. Day one – light dawned. The glory pillar brought Heaven's light upon the nation. What would be their response? Would they worship? Would they pitch a firmament-tabernacle? Would they structure their heaven as the dwelling of God or would they worship a false god, pitch a counterfeit tabernacle, and structure their heaven as the dwelling place of demons? Light dawned and the invitation to abide under an open Heaven was offered to Israel.

Separating the Waters

Within a short time after the Exodus, Pharaoh regretted that he had released his slaves. He gathered his horses and chariots and pursued Israel. The pillar that had been leading the nation lifted up and moved behind the people, thus providing a barrier between the people of God and the forces of Egypt. *"And it came between the camp of the Egyptians and the camp of Israel; and it was a cloud and darkness to them, but it gave light by night to these: so that the one came not near the other all the night."* (Ex. 14:20)

Israel was trapped. The Egyptians were behind them and the Red Sea was before them. God instructed Moses to use his rod, touch the waters, and loose a miracle. Miracles occur when the properties of the spiritual realm are experienced in the physical realm. When Heavenly realities break in upon the earth, laws of another dimension or another sphere are released that supercede earthly, natural laws. Because the unseen existed prior to the seen (II Cor. 4:18) and because what is seen came from the dimension of the unseen (Heb. 11:3), the spiritual laws have superiority over the physical laws. Portals and rods release the higher laws. These events are called miracles.

As Moses stretched his rod over the seas, the waters parted creating a passage on dry ground. Waters heaped on the right and walled high on the left. The ground under the feet of the Israelites was dry. A miracle occurred. An aspect of the eternal realm was temporarily experienced. Heaven and earth harmonized and synchronized to the laws of Heaven. What was impossible in man's world yielded to a superior force, and nature obeyed its Creator. The portal released Heaven on earth.

The waters stayed, allowing every person and beast safe passage. The Egyptians pursued into the water-walled portal where God caused the wheels to fall off of the chariots. Moses stretched forth his rod a second time, and the seas closed in upon the pursuing army. The entire host of Pharaoh was encased in a watery grave. The miraculous deliverance of the servants of God occurred simultaneously with the miraculous destruction of the reprobate servants of the Devil.

All earthly waters on man's side of the firmament are found in two locations. Either they are stored in the clouds or they are located in the rivers, lakes, seas, or oceans. All earthly waters are the same waters, which are just recycled by condensation and rain. It could be stated that the Red Sea was a container for firmament waters. As far back as Adam, fallen man began to corrupt the arrangement of the firmament, thus spiritually contaminating the earthly water supply, which is the force that nourishes the earth. Idol worship continually corrupts the source of life that feeds back into the earth until men are eventually swallowed up by a flood of contaminated waters. Like the men in Noah's day and the soldiers of Pharaoh's army, idol worshippers create the source of their own destruction.

The waters of destruction, or those waters that were formed from altars dedicated to idols, did not destroy God's people. The Israelites were dwelling under another source of water. They moved under the cloud-canopy. They could expect their heaven and earth repositories to contain healthy, life-giving water. Therefore, when they came to the bitter waters at Marah (Ex. 15:23-27), God gave them a tree branch, a symbolic wand, to open a portal to the cleansed heavenly waters. The waters were purified and Israel was nourished. Likewise, when they needed water at Rephidim (Ex. 17:1-7), Moses struck a rock with his rod, opened a portal, and released a miracle; thus life-sustaining waters flowed.

The heavens over the nation distilled life. The waters from the morning dew fell upon the ground. When the dew evaporated, the ground was covered with manna, which was Heaven's bread. From water to drink to manna to eat, from shade by day to fire by night, from miracles in the sky to miracles upon the earth – the portal to God's glory was a covering for the Israelites. And the pillar cloud brought them to the Mountain of God.

Climbing the Mountain of God

In the third month, the glory cloud came to rest upon Mt. Sinai. Sinai is often used interchangeably with Horeb, which is the mountain where God had appeared to Moses in the burning bush and where Moses was instructed to return with the children of Israel. (Ex. 3:1-12; 19:1-2) The portal that opened to Moses at Horeb moved with him to Egypt, overshadowed the nation during the Exodus, guided Israel back to Horeb, and then rested upon the Mountain of God. Moses ascended the mountain to meet with God on several occasions. The following records one of those encounters:

Exodus 24:1, 10-12, 15-18:   *"And he (God) said unto Moses, Come up unto the Lord, thou, and Aaron, Nadab, and Abihu, and seventy of the elders of Israel; and worship ye afar off. . . . And they saw the God of Israel: and there was under his feet as it were a paved work of a sapphire stone, and as it were the body of heaven in his clearness. And upon the nobles of the children of Israel he laid not his hand: also they saw God, and did eat and drink.   And the Lord said unto Moses, Come up to me into the mount, and be there: and I will give thee tables of stone, and a law, and commandments which I have written; that thou mayest teach them. . . . And Moses went up into the mount, and a cloud covered the mount.   And the glory of the Lord abode upon mount Sinai, and the cloud covered it six days: and the seventh day he called unto Moses out of the midst of the cloud.   And the sight of the glory of the Lord was like devouring fire on the top of the mount in the eyes of the children of Israel.   And Moses went into the midst of the cloud, and gat him up into the mount: and Moses was in the mount forty days and forty nights."*

The idea of a mountain as it develops within the context of biblical symbolism is that of a high place upon which man can meet God. In natural creation, the top of the mountain is nearest to Heaven. While existing in the physical dimension, there is no higher standing point for man than the apex of a mountain. Mountain peaks break into the clouds, thus appearing to jut into Heaven. Mountains are likened unto ladders to Heaven by providing man with a way to climb up to God. Therefore, high places are traditionally sites for religious ceremonies and spiritual encounters.

Examples abound in Scripture. Abraham offered Isaac on Mount Moriah. (Gen. 22:2) Elijah defeated Baal on Mount Carmel (I Kin. 18) and received his commission renewed on Mount Sinai. (I Kin. 19) Jesus had several mountaintop experiences: He preached His ultimate sermon on a mount, (Mt. 5) was transfigured on a mount, (II Pet. 1:16-18) and gave His final great commission on a mountain. (Mt. 28:18-20) Christians are to be a city set on a hill that cannot be hidden. (Mt. 5:14) Isaiah 2:2 promises that the day will come when the mountain of the Lord's House will be established as the chief mountain and all nations will stream into it. Daniel foresaw God's holy mountain growing until it filled the whole world. (Dan. 2:34-35)

Mountain symbolism is also found in all world religions. The Hindus have Mount Meru; the Japanese, Fujiyama; and the Greeks, Olympus. Where natural mountains don't exist, men build them. Egypt's pyramids, Indian mounds, or Babylonian ziggurats are all examples of man-made high places. Whoever controls the high places controls the heaven. And, whoever controls the heaven controls the earth. God wanted Israel to control the heaven.

In the event under discussion, Mount Sinai was ablaze with God's presence. A portal was opened, and Moses was invited to draw near and meet God at the top of the mountain. While engulfed in the glory, Moses received instructions on the design of an earthly house wherein God would dwell among the people. Throughout the time of the patriarchs, individuals raised altars upon which they would sacrifice. These altars of worship served to erect a non-visible, firmament-tabernacle in which the glory of God would appear. From Abel's day unto Jacob's day, the practice continued. Jacob revealed that the portal to God's Heaven was one and the same as the house of God, Bethel. However, there was no earthly, visible house of God. That was about to be altered as God introduced the next phase of redemptive history. Moses was instructed to erect a tent as a house for God.

At the base of the mountain, the people wearied waiting for Moses to return. They persuaded Aaron to take their golden jewelry and fashion a golden calf of which they said, *"These be thy gods, O Israel, which brought thee up out of the land of Egypt."* (Ex. 32:4) To this image, they offered sacrifices. Upon the mountain, God instructed Moses to return to the people because they had corrupted themselves. Upon re-entering the camp, Moses cast down and broke the tablets upon which God had written the commandments. He took the calf, melted and ground it, then mixed it in water and caused the Israelites to drink. Moses knew that idol worship corrupted the arrangement of the firmament, thus spiritually contaminating the earthly water supply. If they wanted waters contaminated by idol worship, they would partake of them.

Moses returned before God to make intercession for the people and to repent on behalf of their sin. God responded by granting permission for Moses and the Israelites to continue the journey to the land promised to Abraham. God would send an angel, but God would not journey with them. In essence, the idol worship would have the effect of closing the portal. Heaven and earth would lose the connection. Israel would be separated from the glory. Moses prayed, *"If thy presence go not with me, carry us not up hence."* (Ex. 33:15) God honored the request, allowed the portal to remain open, and invited Moses to again ascend the mountain into the glory.

Pitching a Tent for the Glory

Moses and Israel were commissioned to build a dwelling for God upon the earth. Because God already had a dwelling place in the eternal realm, the pattern of God's house already existed. Moses ascended the mountain to see how things were done in the dimension of God. By constructing an earthly replica of the heavenly prototype, the throne in God's realm would be rebuilt in man's realm. Earth would testify of the realities of God and His ways. Earth would harmonize with Heaven. Earth would again be a welcoming atmosphere for God to dwell among His own in the Tabernacle of Moses. (Please note that the information discussed about Moses' Tabernacle is in context with the subject of portals and is not meant to be a detailed look into all aspects of truth to be gained from a complete study of Exodus 25-31.)

The Tabernacle had three compartments: an Outer Court, a Holy Place, and the Holy of Holies. Processing from east to west, the layout provided steps through which one could approach the glory. The layout was a horizontal Jacob's ladder by which a worshipper could enter from the earthly gate and figuratively ascend to meet God on the other end. The Tabernacle was a continuing picture of Jacob's ladder, a portal, and a Bethel. God was recycling the same message in a new and improved form to be sure that His people knew how to structure their heaven and earth as a dwelling place for God.

Because man could climb up to God's presence through the Tabernacle, it was also a mountain of the Lord. God had brought Israel to Mount Sinai because that mountain would function as a model for the structure Moses was called to build. The base of the mountain had a boundary around it so that the people could not break the protocol of approved procedure to approach God's glory. (Ex. 19:12) The mountain's base corresponded to the Outer Court. The Israelite citizen could approach the Tabernacle, enter the first compartment by the eastern gate, and draw near the first article of furniture, which was the Brazen Altar. At the altar, the priests fulfilled the laws of sacrifice; and the smoke of the burnt offering filled the sky continuously as the substitute sacrifice was offered to atone for the sins of the people and the death sentence incurred by Adam. The courtyard was equivalent to the earthly realm. Beyond the altar, an invisible boundary was set; and the lay Israelite could go no further back into the courtyard.

Behind the Brazen Altar and immediately before entering into the second compartment was a bronze water basin called the Laver. The priests were instructed to wash themselves before they approached the inner court. To approach the Tabernacle's counterpart – the mountain – Moses commanded the priests to sanctify themselves, the same idea as washing.

The second compartment, called the Holy Place was accessible only to the priests. This area contained a table with bread, a lampstand, and an altar upon which incense was burned. The Holy Place had a corresponding area midway up the mountain of Sinai and a corresponding group that were allowed to enter. Only Moses, Aaron, Nadab, Abihu and seventy of the elders of Israel, as representative Levites, were granted permission to approach. Upon the mountain they ate a meal that correlates with the Table of Shewbread. As elders, they were analogous to the Golden Candlestick, because they served as the nation's illumination by allowing God's Word and His Spirit to fuel their leadership and cause them to illuminate the pathway for the people. Finally, the smoke of the glory cloud was associated with the smoke arising from the Altar of Incense.

As the elders entered into the symbolic Holy Place, they saw God through a temporarily transparent veil, which has been discussed earlier as a crystal sea or the waters on top of the firmament. (chapter one) The blue sapphire pavement was equivalent to the veil that separated the Holy Place from the Holy of Holies. The Tabernacle's second compartment corresponded to man's heaven, and the veil marked the firmament-boundary between man's heaven and God's Heaven. The priests entered daily to minister in the Holy Place, but admittance into the Holy of Holies required a special opening, a portal.

Behind the veil was the Ark of the Covenant. Its construction testified that it was God's earthly throne room. His glory came to sit upon a golden lid called the Mercy Seat. Golden cherubim were sculpted and positioned at each end of the Mercy Seat. The imagery of Heaven's golden throne surrounded by angelic hosts is unmistakably reproduced in the Ark. Angels visible in a glory shaft is likewise a revisiting of the theme of Jacob's ladder. At Moses' Tabernacle, God opened a portal that connected Heaven to the Holy of Holies.

Moses was separated from the other leaders and invited to move higher up the mountain and to enter into the presence of God. He alone was granted access to the glory just as later only the High Priest would be granted admission into the Holy of Holies. From the base of the mountain to the middle and on to the summit, Mount Sinai was a model ladder to Heaven reproduced in the Outer Court, Holy Place, and Holy of Holies, respectively, of the Tabernacle of Moses.

Moses came down from the mountain with the pattern and the people built the earthly replica of the Heavenly prototype. When the construction was completed, the glory of God came to rest upon the Tabernacle as it had come to rest upon the Mountain of God. (Ex. 40:33-38) When the people left Mt. Sinai, they took the mountain, a moveable high place, with them. Israel did not need to go back to the mountain after the Tabernacle was built, because the Tabernacle became God's portable mountain. God had given to the nation an open Heaven that would move with them. The nation of replacement 'adams' had fulfilled the day two re-creation pattern. They worshipped. They pitched a firmament-tabernacle in their earthly sphere. They claimed their heaven and earth as a dwelling for God.

CHAPTER FIVE

Aaron: The Instruction for Cloud-Building

Approaching God's Presence

Adam lived under the first open Heaven. His sin caused him to be expelled from God's house. Angels were set at the east of the garden to guard the way. (Gen. 3:24) Access to the Heavenly realm was denied to him. However, God did not recall His Word because of the failure of an 'adam.' God set about to redeem and to restore His purposes for the earth and for mankind. Men were called and given keys to reconnect Heaven and earth. God's glory portal opened over the patriarchs providing temporary doorways to God's Heaven at such places as altars, Jacob's ladder, the burning bush, Moses' rod, the pillar of fire, Mount Sinai, and the Tabernacle of Moses.

Because Moses' Tabernacle was an earthly reproduction of the Mountain of the Lord, the concept of ascending was a predominant theme. The compartments and the furniture were laid out in such a manner that they communicated a patterned approach to the realms of glory. They served as steps or rungs in the ladder. Man was invited to climb. God was dwelling in the midst of His people. (Ex. 25:8) A portal remained open. Just as Jacob had experienced, God was present in the Tabernacle of Moses to release Heaven into the earth. What promises! What power! What possibilities!

The gate to the Tabernacle was set on the east, just as the garden's gate was an eastern gate. The Brazen Altar was positioned immediately inside the gate signifying that the only approach to God was through a substitute sacrifice. As the theme of redemption developed throughout the Scriptures, the New Covenant believer realized that the Brazen Altar testified of the substitutionary work of Jesus. Each step in Moses' Tabernacle was more clearly defined as the New Testament revealed what the Old Testament foreshadowed. (Heb. 10:1) The Brazen Altar spoke of salvation that was available through the blood and provided the first step in approaching God.

The second article was the Laver, which was positioned behind the Brazen Altar and before the door leading to the second compartment, which was called the Holy Place. The sons of Aaron who ministered inside the second area were commanded to stop and wash themselves before conducting inner court ministry. Again drawing from more defined New Testament revelation, the Aaronic and Levitical priests represented the priesthood of all believers (I Pet. 2:9) and the Laver represented the washings or baptisms of regeneration (Tit. 3:5), including water baptism (Rom. 6:4) and the baptism into the body of Christ. (I Cor. 12:13) The Outer Court corresponded to the earthly realm. The works of God the Son, who came to earth to accomplish the redemption of man, are connected to the Outer Court.

Regenerated and cleansed, the Aaronic priests of Moses' day entered the second compartment where more stages of ascent could be found. That area was covered and, thus, not exposed to the light of the sun nor to the view of anyone outside the curtains. As was noted in the previous chapter, the Holy Place corresponded to man's heaven; therefore it represented the spiritual dimension accessible to man and under his stewardship. Spiritual activities take place in the spirit realm. Heavenly activity requires illumination from a non-earthly light source rather than the sun, and spiritual realities originate in the non-visible realm rather than the visible realm. The works of God the Holy Spirit, who was sent to guide, illuminate, and aid earthly believers to live like heavenly people, are connected to the Inner Court.

The first article of furniture was the Golden Candlestick, which was filled with oil and provided light for the Holy Place. Again drawing from more developed revelation found in the New Testament, the lampstand represented an appointed vessel, such as Jesus who was the light of the world, a particular church like those addressed in chapters two and three of Revelation, or the believers who are lights set on a hill. These lampstands shine truth because of the Word and the anointing oil of the Holy Spirit.

To the right of the lamp was the Table of Shewbread. The Bible commands the believer to ingest the Word, which came from Heaven in the form of manna, Jesus as the bread of Heaven, or the recorded cannon of Scripture. Saints become transformed into citizens of Heaven by eating Heaven's bread.

Filled with the Spirit and the Word, the priest was ready to approach the golden Altar of Incense. Incense, whose formula was God-given and which composition was not to be altered, was placed upon coals that were carried from the Brazen Altar and used as the source of fire in the golden altar. The incense corresponded to prayers and worship. *"Let my prayer be set forth before thee as incense; and the lifting up of my hands as the evening sacrifice."* (Ps. 141:2) The activity of worship-offering, prayer-entreating, and incense-burning was done in the area that corresponded to man's heaven. Because worship is the deed that erects the firmament-tabernacle, the priest was structuring the heaven over Israel by the spiritual activity accomplished at the Altar of Incense.

Directly in front of the golden altar stood a veil embroidered with cherubim that served as a partition between the Holy Place and the Holy of Holies. (Ex. 26:31-33) The veil represented the firmament that was erected to divide man's heaven from God's Heaven. Pre-fall there was a firmament, but it did not exclude man from God's realm nor did it act as a barrier between God and man. Post-fall, the firmament closed. Access to God's realm was denied. Therefore, inside the Tabernacle, cherubim were placed upon the veil to remind the priests of Moses' day that Adam had been cast away from an open Heaven and that God had set angels to guard His glory realm. The New Testament believer is afforded approach to God through a torn veil, the implications of which will be explored in chapter nine.

Beyond the veil was the Holy of Holies, which represented the upper side of the firmament or God's Heaven. There, on a golden throne encompassed by angels, which was called the Ark of the Covenant, the manifest presence of God resided. The throne in the highest Heaven was reproduced in the earthly Holy of Holies. As the glory cloud filled God's Heavenly throne room, so did the glory cloud fill the throne room of Moses' Tabernacle. One time each year the high priest was allowed to enter with the blood of a substitute. The New Testament fully unveiled that Jesus was the high priest who entered into God's throne with His own blood. This He did one time to atone for man's sin. (Heb. 9:23-24)

Thus, the steps to approach the glory were outlined in the Tabernacle of Moses. From salvation to walking in the Spirit, from learning about God to experiencing the glory of God, from the earthly base of a portal to the

Heavenly opening of that portal, God's people could ascend, could connect, could dwell under an open Heaven. As with all 'adams,' worship and obedience would guarantee an atmosphere for an open portal.

Building an Atmosphere for the Glory

The main replacement 'adam,' upon which the Scriptures focus in connection with Tabernacle ministry is Aaron. Aaron was the brother of Moses. Aaron is introduced at the time that Moses was summoned at the burning bush. Fearful that he was inadequate to fluently speak the dialects of either the Hebrews or the Egyptians after so long an absence, Moses entreated God to send another to interpret and aid him in his communication. God sent Aaron. Moses would hear from God and impart God's instruction to Aaron, then Aaron would speak for Moses.

Aaron and Moses worked together throughout the contest with Pharaoh, and Aaron was often the one who wielded the rod that released Heaven's power through the portal. On the negative side, Aaron was cooperative with the people in the golden calf incident and facilitated them in the use of idolatrous patterns learned from Egypt rather than leading them in acceptable worship patterns given by Jehovah. While Moses was upon the mountain receiving the instruction for the Tabernacle, Aaron was in charge of the leaders who encamped midway up the mount.

The above mentioned incidents were training grounds for the priestly office into which Aaron was called. Because the Tabernacle was a working portal to Heaven, Aaron's early experience with Moses' rod familiarized him with portals and God's power. Because Aaron was mandated to lead the nation into tabernacle worship, his incident with the calf must have firmly imprinted him with the danger of counterfeit worship. And finally, because Aaron was appointed as the chief priest, the position of authority afforded him as Moses' representative served to validate his leadership among the people.

As high priest, Aaron was responsible to create and maintain an atmosphere for the glory. Just as Adam had the power to re-create Heaven on the earth by following God's three-day pattern, Aaron was afforded a similar duty. God spoke. Day one broke in upon Aaron. The light of Heaven dawned when the tabernacle pattern was given and Aaron was set aside to fulfill his mandate. Moses' Tabernacle was a replacement 'garden of eden' and Aaron was a replacement 'adam'. Both had been identified. Aaron had to work to structure man's heaven so as to guarantee a Heavenized earth.

Inside the inner court was the replica of man's heaven. As has been stated, the veil was the point of separation, or the metaphoric firmament, between man's heaven and God's Heaven. On God's side of the veil was glory. Aaron was given the task of making an atmosphere whereby God's glory was also present on man's side of the firmament symbolically found inside the Holy Place.

Glory descended upon Mt. Sinai and the phenomena of the glory was as the appearance of smoke, fire, and light. When God's glory was in man's heaven at the Exodus, it was a cloud by day and a fire by night. Therefore, if God's glory were manifest in the inner court of the Tabernacle, one would expect the properties to remain consistent with other appearances. Where smoke, fire, and light found in the Holy Place? They were!

As the priest offered incense upon the Golden Altar, a cloud was created. The prescribed mixture of spices was thrown upon hot coals, which resulted in the formation of an incense cloud mixed with fiery sparks from the coals. As the altar was located immediately in front of the veil, the fire-filled smoke arose to fill the inner court. However, because smoke is a vapor, it is reasonable to assume that some of the incense cloud seeped around and over the veil into the Holy of Holies where the glory cloud resided. The clouds may have co-mingled. Although the thought of both clouds converging is speculation, the Scripture clearly states that on the Day of Atonement, the High Priest took a censer of incense behind the veil for the prescribed purpose of the cloud of incense covering the Mercy Seat. (Lev. 16:13) If the incense merged with the glory on the Day of Atonement and because the veil did not provide a tightly-sealed barrier, it is reasonable to assume that the incense cloud on man's side mixed with the glory cloud on God's side. The penetration of the cloud through the veil communicated a pattern for opening a portal into God's Heaven. Whether or not the clouds literally converged, the imagery is still clear.

Clouds on man's side of the veil depicted clouds in man's heaven. At Sinai, clouds of glory rested upon the mountaintop. Because the Tabernacle of Moses was an earthly reproduction of the Mountain of the Lord, the concept of clouds was a predominant theme. The altar was the counterpart of the mountain's peak that appeared to penetrate Heaven. Realizing that the altar was the piece of tabernacle furniture placed nearest to Holy of Holies or at the point of entrance into God's glory realm reinforces the concept. The Altar of Incense was the metaphoric summit of the mountain upon which the cloud resided.

At Sinai, God was in the cloud that rested in man's heaven. As the priest created the cloud of incense, he was structuring man's heaven after the pattern of God's Heaven. The glory cloud around the throne was being re-created under the firmament-tabernacle called the veil. Prior to the fall, the waters above the firmament were identical to the waters under the firmament. Aaron was instructed to create identical waters or vapors of clouds. The principle emerges: when man's heaven and God's Heaven match, God moves into the heaven man has prepared for Him.

Riding on the Clouds

God sits enthroned upon the clouds that are created by worship. Psalm 104:3 says that He makes the clouds His chariot. The idea of a cloud-chariot is found in several passages in the Scriptures. Isaiah told of a heavenly worship service that created such a cloud.

Isaiah 6:1-4: *"In the year that king Uzziah died I saw also the Lord sitting upon a throne, high and lifted up, and his train filled the temple. Above it stood the seraphims: each one had six wings; with twain he covered his face, and with twain he covered his feet, and with twain he did fly. And one cried unto another, and said, Holy, holy, holy, is the Lord of hosts: the whole earth is full of his glory. And the posts of the door moved at the voice of him that cried, and the house was filled with smoke."*

The scene occurred on God's side of the firmament. Angels were crying *"holy, holy, holy"* around the throne, which was the seat where God's glory resided. In the midst of God's manifested Heavenly glory, the seraphim worshipped. The doorposts and thresholds of the entryway began to vibrate by a phenomenon created by the angels' voices. Next, the whole house was filled with smoke. The glory that rested upon the throne took wings on the praises of the angels and moved out through a doorway or portal to fill the chambers outside of the throne room. The imagery is clear. God will ride or be enthroned upon a cloud created by worship.

The Ark of the Covenant, where the glory 'sat' on the wings of the cherubim, was called a chariot of the cherubim. (I Chr. 28:18) Ezekiel built upon the concept of an angelic cloud-chariot as he described a glory cart created by four cherubim. The prophet told how the glory lifted from the Ark and moved over to sit upon the angelic cloud-chariot, which provided transportation for the glory. (Ez. 9-11)

God was transported over angels' wings, or it could be said that He was carried upon the shoulders of His messengers. Although Ezekiel and Isaiah describe how God moved by means of His angels, Scriptures also define how God moves on man's side of the firmament by other 'angels'. Mankind is the earthly counterpart to the angels in Heaven. Angels are the envoys to carry God's decrees just as men are messengers of the good news. Angels worship in Heaven. People worship on earth. God is glorified by the hosts of Heaven and by the inhabitants of the earth. King David discovered that the only acceptable transportation system for God's glory must follow the Heavenly pattern. God rides upon the shoulders of His messengers. (I Chr. 15:2)

Psalm 22:3 says that God sits enthroned upon the praises of His people. Praise creates a cloud. Remembering that the burning of incense was a cloud-building activity and that incense represented worship and prayer (Rev. 5:8; 8:3; Ps. 141:2), the premise emerges that praise and prayer rise to create the glory cloud which God will inhabit on man's side of the firmament. Common phrases are used to verify the ascending nature of praise and prayer. Believers are called to lift their voices in praise or to offer up their prayers. Even given the natural conditions of cold air temperatures, man's very breath is made visible as a vapor, further verifying that the spoken word has the ability to form a cloud.

Aaron and his sons were commanded to offer incense, which pictured worship and prayer. A cloud was created like the cloud of glory. Man's heaven was structured after the pattern of God's Heaven and a welcoming atmosphere was created for the glory. Aaron improved upon the second day firmament-building worship that was offered by Adam on his second day. Adam gave God no worship, created no cloud-chariot for the glory, and offered no shoulders upon which glory could move into man's heaven. Aaron succeeded where Adam failed. In fact, years later, the lineage of Aaron was still faithfully offering incense. In one particular example, a man by the name of Zacharias, whose wife was a direct descendant of Aaron, was fulfilling the priestly duty of building a cloud-chariot when a portal opened and an angel appeared. (Lk.1:5-20)

Piercing the Heaven

The principle of worship creating a seat upon which an exalted one is elevated is not uncommon. Champions are lifted upon the shoulders of the adoring crowds. The victor's name is chanted as if to raise his achievements and his person into a lofty and predominant level. The one being praised is elevated and paraded around in the adoration of the worshippers. This principle is so powerful that Satan coveted God's position of riding on the shoulders of the angels and the cloud-chariot they formed.

Isaiah 14:13-14: *"For thou hast said in thine heart, I will ascend into heaven, I will exalt my throne above the stars of God: I will sit also upon the mount of the congregation, in the sides of the north: I will ascend above the heights of the clouds; I will be like the most High."*

He enticed one-third of the host to attempt to create a chariot in his honor. God did not permit counterfeit worship in His Heaven. The serpent came to Adam and Eve. Would the angelic counterpart on earth build a cloud-chariot for the Devil? Would they enthrone him on their praises? Certainly they did. The incense they offered created a cloud upon which demonic forces could ride, thus man's heaven became the habitation of fallen angelic beings. In context with this, Moses' admonition to Aaron was that the priests could offer no strange incense upon the golden altar nor could they use strange fire. When Aaron's sons, Nadab and Abihu, built a counterfeit cloud, they were destroyed. (Lev. 10:1-3) God was communicating that counterfeit cloud-building has no place in man's heaven.

Satanically-occupied heavens created a barrier between man and the throne of God. Yet, God provided means by which faithful worshippers could pierce the second heaven and open a portal for God to move into man's realm. As Aaron was faithful at the Altar of Incense, the cloud filled the inner court. The veil that separated man and God became obscured as the priest viewed it through the incense cloud. Depending upon the density and brightness of the cloud, the barrier disappeared, if only momentarily. The idea was communicated that the barrier could be thinned or pierced, thus releasing things locked up in God's realm.

An angel was released to Zacharias, but he was not the only example. Scripture tells of Daniel who prayed at the set time of evening when the incense was scheduled to be burned. While he was praying, the angel Gabriel appeared to release to him revelation about future truths that had been sealed in God's counsel. (Dan. 9:20-23) Daniel began to seek God for understanding of the words. After twenty-one days of prayer, Daniel pierced the Heaven. (Dan. 10:12-13) Another Heavenly visitor appeared to Daniel who explained that he had been delayed because of the demonically-structured heaven over Persia. Daniel's altar of incense, cloud-building, barrier-piercing prayer ministry had prevailed and a portal was opened for Heaven to break through.

Without the altar of incense ministry that structures man's heaven for God, the satanically-structured heaven prevails. When replacement 'adams' such as Aaron faithfully attend to God's altars, the demonically-infested heaven looses power. Glory-chariots are created through the incense of worship and prayer. Firmament-barriers are pierced. Portals are opened. God's glory appears in man's heaven. Let God arise and let His enemies be scattered! (Ps. 68:1)

CHAPTER SIX

Elijah: The Responsibility to Control Altars

Contesting for Control

Altars are the meeting place of two domains. They are the connecting points. They open the portals. A human 'adam' stands at the earthly base. His purpose is to bring the power and the presence of another dimension into his mortal realm. A spiritual entity stands at the heavenly opening. The deity's purpose is to release his power and agenda into the affairs of earth. If the human agent is godly and the deity is the Lord, the altar blesses the earth by channeling things locked up in God's highest Heaven. If the human agent is ungodly and the deity is satanic, the altar curses the earth by channeling things contained within the demonically-structured heaven. Therefore, earth is blessed or cursed at altars; angels or demons are released at altars; the Creator or destroyer is empowered at altars.

Altars have attendants in both spheres. The agent who raised the earthly altar functions as a priest or gatekeeper to keep the portal open. The deity to whom the altar was dedicated becomes the supervising spirit or gatekeeper to the spirit's domain. The priest seeks to download something. When the altar is raised to the Lord, man wants the righteous ways of God and the glory of His kingdom. When the altar is raised to another god, man wants to funnel supernatural power such as assistance in battle, the cooperation of elements for growing crops, knowledge of the unknown, or wealth and fame. In each case, the priest of the altar seeks to draw strength from the god.

The supervising spirit also has an agenda. Because the earth was originally granted to the authority of man (Ps. 8; 115:16), heavenly powers league with human agents for legal ground to access earth. God advances His kingdom through His redeemed, and Satan advances his kingdom through his representatives. Two kingdoms are in conflict. Two deities want man's authority. Two rival priesthoods service diversely opposing altars to facilitate the agendas of distinctly conflicting spirits.

Because the priest and the supervising spirit both have agendas, altars become places where leagues are made. Both parties want a form of power. Man wants supernatural intervention. The deity wants human authority. Contracts or covenants are made. God cuts covenant. His covenants are holy and filled with promises that heavenly assets will be available to the man who releases His will in the earth. The Devil, who counterfeits the ways of God, also cuts covenants. His covenants are unholy; and although filled with promises for power to those who release his will in the earth, his covenants come with the price of eternal damnation to any that follow him.

Thus, an altar can be defined as follows: An altar is a place of spiritual power that is attended by an earthly priesthood who draws strength from the spirit that supervises the altar. Conversely, an altar is a place of spiritual power that is supervised by a spirit that releases other-worldly agendas through the altar's earthly priesthood.

Because men want to control their circumstances and because spirits want to control men, altars become portals for control. Men seek to control the land and those who live on it. Spirits seek to control the land and those who live on it. Man's authority and spirit's power converge at altars to control all that dwell in the sphere of influence of that priest and that supervising spirit. An altar can affect a family, a community, or a nation. The rank of the deity and degree of the covenant determine the parameters of the altar's influence.

Whoever dwells under a portal created by an altar will come under the persuasion of the god to whom the altar was dedicated. For example, Jacob did not know that his grandfather had raised an altar at Bethel; but when Jacob laid down to rest upon the land, he came under the power of the God to whom Abraham had dedicated the altar. Conversely, when the priests of Israel allowed altars to satanic powers to be erected, the inhabitants departed from the law of God and practiced all manner of abomination.

God had warned Israel about the land He promised to give to them. It was filled with idol worshippers. Israel was to destroy the altars that had been erected to the satanic deities so that the nation would not come under the power of demonic influence. God mandated:

Deuteronomy 7:1-2, 5-6: *"When the Lord thy God shall bring thee into the land whither thou goest to possess it, and hath cast out many nations before thee, the Hittites, and the Girgashites, and the Amorites, and the Canaanites, and the Perizzites, and the Hivites, and the Jebusites, seven nations greater and mightier than thou; And when the Lord thy God shall deliver them before thee; thou shalt smite them, and utterly destroy them; thou shalt make no covenant with them, nor shew mercy unto them: . . . . But thus shall ye deal with them; ye shall destroy their altars, and break down their images, and cut down their groves, and burn their graven images with fire. For thou art an holy people unto the Lord thy God: the Lord thy God hath chosen thee to be a special people unto himself, above all people that are upon the face of the earth."*

The degree of obedience of God's people to destroy altars determined the degree of demonic influence over the nation. To be free to obey God, Israel had to contest with idolatrous altars. During times when the land was cleansed of altars, national revival resulted. During seasons of coexistence with idolatrous altars, spiritual and social deterioration occurred. The book of Judges chronicles the ebb and flow of Israel's willingness to contest for control over altars.

In the days of the zenith of Israel's power, King Solomon disobeyed God's Law and entered into many matrimonial alliances with surrounding nations. One result of his many marriages was the introduction of idol worship practiced by his wives. (I Kin. 11:1-10; II Kin. 23:13) High places were built to service supervising spirits named Chemosh – god of the Moabites, Milcom – god of the Ammonites, and Baal and Ashtoreth – god and goddess of the Zidonians.

After the death of Solomon, the nation divided under two different kings. Ten tribes in the northern part of the land followed Jeroboam, became known as Israel, and moved the capitol city to Shechem. The two remaining tribes followed Rehoboam, the son of Solomon, became known as Judah, and kept the capitol in Jerusalem. Jeroboam was known for perverting God's revealed patterns given to Moses. He changed the lineage of the priests, altered the holy days, and made Bethel the holy city to insure that the citizens would not migrate to Jerusalem to worship and thus come under the influence of that Heavenly portal. (I Kin. 12:25-33) He set up counterfeit altars and erected golden calves in both Dan and Bethel, for which God judged him and disqualified his sons from becoming heirs to the throne. (I Kin. 14:7-11) Although his lineage was severed, his idolatrous influence continued.

The seventh monarch of Israel's Northern Kingdom was King Ahab who married Jezebel, the daughter of Ethbaal the priest-king of Zidon. She gave open endorsement for the worship of the Phoenician god Baal and the female deity Ashtoreth (at times recorded as Asherah). Ahab and Jezebel serviced the altars of Baal and Ashtoreth, respectively, thus releasing the supervising spirits to dramatically affect the lives of the citizenry. Four hundred and fifty priests of Baal and four hundred priests of Ashtoreth, who ate at Jezebel's table, were empowered to erect and maintain altars to these demon gods.

Into that scene of witchcraft and idolatry, Scripture introduced the prophet Elijah. Israel had abandoned the altar and the priestly stipulations about which Moses had instructed Aaron. Satanic altars had been raised. Satanic priests were servicing altars dedicated to satanic deities. The people were dwelling under the a demonically-structured heaven and were influenced by ruling spirits released through the counterfeit altars. Elijah appeared to contest for control of earth's altars.

Closing the Windows of Heaven

Elijah must have been functioning as a prophet and building his reputation as a man of God before his introduction in I Kings. No details of his background are stated. He just appeared and announced to King Ahab that there would be a drought. *"As the Lord God of Israel liveth, before whom I stand, there shall not be dew nor rain these years, but according to my word."* (I Kin. 17:1) Elijah stated that the heaven would be closed and would not open over Israel until he declared.

Understanding of Elijah's proclamation concerning sealed-off heavenly waters can be discovered by a brief review of principles discussed earlier in this manuscript. Recall that on God's second day of creation, He placed a barrier or a firmament between the waters above and the waters below. All the waters that had resided in one source prior to the firmament were identical in properties after the firmament-barrier. Man was set as appointed vice-regent of the earthly sphere, which included man's heaven and man's earth. Therefore, man was responsible to keep the

118

waters in his heaven harmonious with the waters in God's Heaven.

Man's waters are natural, such as those that can be found in earthly containers like lakes or oceans and in heavenly cloud containers. Man's waters also have a spiritual counterpart, which means the natural is a metaphor for the spiritual. Spiritually speaking, clouds are manifestations of God's glory as when the cloud descended upon Mt. Sinai.

Through Moses, Aaron was instructed in cloud-building at the golden altar. Vapors of worship and prayer are to be released from another repository of water, which is man. (Jn. 4:14; 7:38) As in the natural, so in the spiritual. When worship vapors ascend, a cloud canopy is formed; and rains of blessing distill upon the earth. A cloud-filled heaven causes the earth to be fruitful.

Idol worship contaminates the vapors and pollutes the earthly waters, both naturally at times and spiritually at all times. Adam's idolatry disrupted the blessing of Heaven. Adam cast a hardened shell, a rock solid canopy, so to speak. Adam's firmament removed him from the glory cloud and from the blessing that would distill upon his earth. Concepts like barren ground, wilderness lands, and desert conditions were post-garden and post-fall earthly environments.

Moses used the language of a brass or iron heaven to describe the result of idol worship. If Israel persisted in building a closed off Heaven, they would suffer the effects of drought. *"But if ye will not hearken unto me, and will not do all these commandments; And if ye shall despise my statutes, or if your soul abhor my judgments, so that ye will not do all my commandments, but that ye break my covenant: . . . I will break the pride of your power; and I will make your heaven as iron, and your earth as brass."* (Lev. 26:14-15, 19) Conversely, if they honored the altars through obedience to the covenant, *"the Lord shall open unto thee his good treasure, the heaven to give the rain unto thy land in his season."* (Deut. 28:12)

The prophet Elijah spoke the sanctions of God's Word. The altars of Baal and Ashtoreth had created a rock solid firmament sealing up the inhabitants under control of those supervising satanic deities. Elijah knew that the rains of God would not be released until the Devil's altars were destroyed and the demonically-structured heaven was penetrated. He was willing to take responsibility for his land and the altars that had been erected. He was confident that God's altars had ability to release God's power in the earth. Hence, he declared, *"As the Lord God of Israel liveth, before whom I stand, there shall not be dew nor rain these years, but according to my word."* (I Kin. 17:1)

Providing for the Prophet

After his bold proclamation to the powerful king, Elijah was commanded to go to the Brook Cherith. His location was concealed from Ahab and Jezebel. There, God miraculously supplied food through ravens; and there, Elijah undoubtedly renewed his covenant, maintained an open portal, and grew stronger in Heaven's power. God proved that His power and provision were sufficient for Elijah during the days of seclusion in the land promised to Abraham. Although the heirs of Abraham who lived in Elijah's day had forsaken the covenants of their forefather and had worshipped foreign gods, God had provided evidence of His presence to His prophet. Elijah's portal had the power to pierce Israel's demon-infested heaven. His earthly environment yielded blessing to him. Heaven dropped down provision.

When the lack of rain caused the brook to dry up, God sent Elijah to Zidon. Zidon was the homeland of

Queen Jezebel. Zidon was native soil of Baal and Ashtoreth religion. False altars abounded. False priests were throughout the land. Zidon was under the domain of strong demonic influence. Why would God cause the prophet to seek refuge in Zidon?

This Scripture does not clearly state the reason for placing Elijah in that land but does specifically declare the results of his presence. He was sent to the house of a widow. (I Kin. 17:9) She was at the end of her provision with only enough oil and meal for one last morsel of food for her and her son. Elijah instructed her to feed him first; and by doing so, her supplies would be continuous until the drought and famine came to an end. The power of provision moved with the prophet from the land of Israel to the land of foreign deities.

God was again providing evidence. The satanically-structured strongholds of Baal and Ashtoreth over Zidon would have been more powerful and more ancient than their counterparts in Israel. In spite of increased opposition, Elijah's portal had the power to pierce the Zidonian heaven. The widow came under the influence of Elijah's God and had the faith to believe the word of the man of God. From ravens to a widow, God not only provided food but also provided evidence of the power of Heaven that was being released through Elijah's portal. Before the famine ended, the widow's son died; and Elijah's portal supported the ultimate test of a conduit between the two realms. Elijah raised the boy from the dead. The power of the prophet's portal had been tested. The faith of the prophet had been tried. God had prepared His man for the contest that would ensue. At the end of three years, God spoke, *"Go, show thyself to Ahab; and I will send rain upon the earth."* (I Kin. 18:1)

Opening the Windows of Heaven

Elijah summoned the king. Although Ahab was unlikely to be responsive to the directive of one of his citizens, his anger with the prophet prompted him to arise and go to Elijah. Upon approaching the man of God, Ahab retorted, *"Art thou he that troubles Israel?"* (I Kin. 18:17) In other words, Ahab was placing the blame for the drought squarely at the feet of Elijah. Elijah denied culpability but turned the fault back to Ahab and Ahab's royal lineage that had caused Israel to forsake God and follow Baal.

As though the verbal contest with the king was inadequate to satisfy the boldness of the prophet, Elijah called for four hundred and fifty prophets of Baal and four hundred prophets of Ashtoreth to convene upon Mt. Carmel. The citizens also gathered; and to them Elijah issued one more challenge, *"How long will you waver between two opinions? If the Lord is God, follow him; but if Baal is God, follow him."* (I Kin. 18:21, NIV)

The priests of Baal prepared a sacrifice and called upon their deity to send fire from heaven upon the offering. They petitioned Baal from morning till noon. Upon the chiding of Elijah, they intensified their requests by lacerating their own flesh, which indicated an elevated level of dedication and covenant with the devils. With all the prophesying to the altar, no deity released any manifestation from the spiritual realm. The portal at their altar appeared to have been either closed or obstructed by Elijah's portal.

Elijah went to work. He had to repair the altar of Israel as it had been left without a priestly representative to attend to it. He took twelve stones, one for each tribe of Israel with whom God had cut covenant, and built an altar in the name of the Lord. He commanded that four barrels of water drench the sacrifice and altar. He required this be done three times until the water filled the large trench that he had dug around the altar's base.

Then at the time of the evening sacrifice, the time when the offering was scheduled to ascend before the Lord, the time appointed in the Law, he called on the God of Abraham, Isaac, and Israel. He re-activated the covenant and altars made by the forefathers. He rehearsed the leagues that had opened portals in days gone by. Elijah requested a firmament change, which would release the citizens from Baal's influence and free their hearts to turn back to the covenant of their fathers. (Mal. 4:5-6) He stood at the earthly base of his altar and sought to download power from the Deity who resided on the top of the portal. Heaven opened. God answered by fire. Fire fell and consumed the sacrifice, the wood, the water, and the stones of the altar.

The people responded, *"The LORD, he is the God; the LORD, he is the God."* (I Kin. 18:39b) The rank of the deity and degree of the covenant determine the parameters of the altar's influence. Israel's God far outranked Baal. The covenant made between God and Israel was superior to the league between Baal and his prophets. Elijah's altar had more influence over the people than did Baal's. The people turned their hearts to acknowledge God.

At Elijah's command, the prophets of Baal were rounded up and slaughtered at the base of Carmel at the Kishon River. The blood of the prophets would have undoubtedly filled the basins of the river that flowed along the northern side of the city of Jezreel, which was the residence of Jezebel and Ahab. Eventually the Kishon emptied into the Mediterranean, the Sea Coast along which Zidon was located. The cities and the leaders responsible for the contaminated waters over Israel would be recipients of the blood-polluted waters that their worship had generated.

Elijah returned to Mt. Carmel where he fell on his face to seek God for rain. Elijah had saturated God's altar with water; so that when the offering went up, the vapors from the altar would seed the skies. He knew the principle. Vapors up; rains down. He knew that acceptable worship opens Heaven. He knew that the brass heaven formed by satanic worship had been penetrated. He expected rain. He sent his servant to observe the skies seven times. On the seventh time, the servant returned to report the small wisp of vapors arising from the sea. From the small beginning, the skies turned black with clouds and wind; and there was a great rain in Israel.

Overcoming the Retaliation

Jezebel was furious. She sent word to Elijah that he would be dead by that same time the next day. The man of power fled for his life, traveled a day's journey alone into a wilderness, and requested of God that he could die. Elijah's boldness seemed to have melted like the brass heaven had at Carmel.

Clearly, Elijah had destroyed the four hundred and fifty prophets of the male deity Baal. However, Scripture makes no reference to what happened to the four hundred prophets of female deity Ashtoreth who were also summoned to Mt. Carmel. Perhaps the prophets of both Baal and Ashtoreth were included in the Scriptures' meaning of the prophets of Baal. In that case, all who worked Jezebel's witchcraft would also have been eliminated. If Ashtoreth's prophets were untouched, they could have regrouped, gone to other altars at other locations, and empowered themselves. However, with or without her prophets, Jezebel was a sorceress and an embodiment of the spirit of the queen of heaven, a principle deity of the Phoenicians. (Jer. 7:18; 44:17-25)

Jezebel threatened Elijah with both human and supernatural retaliation. Retaliation from demonic spirits can be real and can be deadly. God hid Moses from Pharaoh's soldiers. The angel told Mary and Joseph to take Baby Jesus to Egypt to avoid Herod. The Book of Revelation depicts a woman who birthed a boy, representative of Christ, who was appointed to rule all nations. (Rev. 12) The scene unfolds to find a dragon, representative of the Devil, unleashing a destroying flood to take vengeance upon the woman; but the earth opens its mouth and swallows up the flood. Although all the symbolism of the passage is beyond the scope of this text, the point remains that the Devil seeks to retaliate. His power is real and his retaliation is dangerous. But, God provided an escape for Moses, Baby Jesus, and the woman of Revelation.

God likewise provided a place of safety for Elijah. God did several things to protect and strengthen His servant. First, He sent Elijah unto Horeb, the Mountain of God. There, in the portal that had been opened to Moses, God unveiled a new revelation of Himself to Elijah. (I Kin.

19:11-18)   Protected by the portal and engulfed in the glory, Elijah was recharged, refocused, and commissioned again.   Secondly, God told Elijah that there were seven thousand who could unify against Baal and rally on behalf of the God of Israel.   Elijah was not alone.   Numbers function to exponentially release power. (Deut. 31:30)   The seven thousand who attended God's altars were more in number than the priests of Baal and Ashtoreth combined. God affirmed His power base.   Along with the knowledge of these faithful, Elijah was told to identify and appoint those who would continue his battle.

Portals are not only places of empowerment, they are also places of safety.   Moses described a secret place under the shadow of the Almighty. (Ps. 91)   The Lord's Shadow was well known to Moses.   It was His glory cloud. It was a portal.   In the threat of various calamities, the portal protects.   In the danger by day or by night, the portal shields.   If a thousand fall on the left and ten thousand on the right, the portal safeguards.   In this portal, the hosts of angels are dispatched to assist.   From the power of the portal, one may walk upon or defeat the serpent spirit that poisons and the lion devil that devours.   Portals protect. Moses knew it well.   Elijah discovered the same truth.

Jezebel's threats, like the prophets' altars, were powerless against a portal opened to God.

CHAPTER SEVEN

Daniel: The Authorization to Pierce the Heaven

Continuing Idolatry

False altars defile. They are places that give authority for satanic forces to be enthroned in man's heaven, and they are places that open doorways for those same satanic forces to invade the earth and influence mankind. Elijah was a mighty prophet. He understood the importance of altars in the land.

Elijah not only defeated the altar of Baal at Carmel and destroyed the false prophets, he also released a word of judgment against Ahab and Jezebel, who were undoubtedly the human embodiment of Baal and Ashtoreth, satanic ruling spirits. Both wicked rulers were destroyed as Elijah had predicted, but the ruling spirits that motivated the monarchs' actions were not eliminated at the death of the hosts. Paul affirms that the battle is not against flesh and blood but against satanic forces that rule from man's heaven. (Eph. 6:12)

Upon the death of Ahab and Jezebel, the devils sought new vessels that would attend the altars and through whom evil agendas could be unleashed upon the citizens of the earth. The lineage of the kings of Israel, which was the Northern Kingdom that had torn from David under Jeroboam, supplied the human instruments. The Bible does not record one Israelite king that instituted spiritual reforms but frequently states of Israel's kings that they *"did that which was evil in the sight of the Lord, and followed the sins of Jeroboam the son of Nebat, which made Israel to sin; he departed not therefrom."* (II Kin. 13:2, 11; 14:24; 15:9, 18, 28)

During the reign of King Hoshea, the Assyrians under King Shalmaneser invaded Israel and carried the people away to captivity. (II Kin. 17:1-6) Scripture testifies that the continual burning of incense in high places unto idols and the use of satanic, occult practices was the cause of the deportation. (II Kin. 17:7-23) Because Israel did not structure their heaven by God's pattern, they lost their authority both in heaven and in earth. They, like Adam, were expelled from the land where God had chosen to make His glory known.

The history of the kings of Judah, which was the Southern Kingdom that followed Solomon's son Rehoboam, had seasons of turning from idol worship. Asa, Jehoshaphat, Amaziah, Uzziah, Jotham, and Josiah were kings of Davidic lineage who brought various levels of cleansing from idolatrous practices and who restored the altars of the Lord. Yet the work was always less than complete, as either high places were allowed to remain or an heir reversed the reforms.

Hezekiah was a good king that *"did right in the sight of the Lord, according to all that David his father did."* (II Kin. 18:3) He removed high places, believed God to rescue Judah against the ominous threats of the king of Assyria, and had fifteen years added to his life because of his fervent prayer. However, pride caused him to unveil all his treasures to the king of Babylon. Isaiah the prophet declared unto him, *"Behold, the days come, that all that is in thine house, and that which thy fathers have laid up in store unto this day, shall be carried into Babylon: nothing shall be left, saith the Lord."* (II Kin. 20:17) Hezekiah responded that it was good that he could have peace in his day and that the judgments would not come until his heirs began their reign.

His son, Manasseh, rebuilt the high places, built altars to idols in God's house, used wizards and occult practices, and did more abominations than the nations whom the Lord destroyed before the children of Israel. God declared His wrath and His judgment upon Judah. *"Behold, I am bringing such evil upon Jerusalem and Judah, that whosoever heareth of it, both his ears shall tingle."* (II Kin. 21:12) After a temporary postponement of the judgment because of the good king Josiah, God fulfilled His Word. Nebuchadnezzer, King of Babylon, besieged the city, deported its citizens, took captive Judah's king, spoiled the treasures of the temple and palace, destroyed both buildings, and tore down the walls of the city.

The protection of the portal afforded Elijah was not available to Judah. God's portal opens the holiness of Heaven upon the earth. Idol worship defiles the altar; sin defiles the holy; iniquity defiles the portal. God's portal closes over those who defile. When Pharaoh's army stepped into the portal at the Red Sea, it closed upon the unholy. They were destroyed. When King Uzziah intruded into the portal at the Altar of Incense, he was unconsecrated and thus emerged as one symbolically dead with leprosy. (I Chr. 16-20)

God's portals are for the traffic of angels, for the presence of glory, for the power of the eternal realm. God closed His portal over corrupt Judah. They lost their protection. They were carried to Babylon.

Locating a New Altar

God did not need a literal house to open a portal. The patriarchs experienced portals prior to Moses' Tabernacle and Solomon's Temple. Elijah dwelt under a portal at the Brook Cherith, in Zidon, on Mt. Carmel, and at Mt. Horeb. A portal opens over an altar, whether that altar is under the open sky, inside a tabernacle, or in a foreign land. God moved His portal to Babylon.

Ezekiel was appointed a prophet to the exiles. He reminded the captives of the national sins that caused the deportation; he sustained their faith by prophecies of restoration; and he announced God's judgments upon nations that sinned against God. God granted Ezekiel great revelations, many of which were spoken in symbolic language or parabolic actions. God also showed Ezekiel the location of His glory in the land of Judah's captivity.

In chapters 9 through 11, Ezekiel described four cherubim that created a chariot with four wheels. One wheel was by each cherub. The glory lifted from its resting place over the Ark in the Holy of Holies and moved to the four-wheeled cherubim cart. Scripture twice described the glory as resting above or over the wheeled cherubim. (Ez. 10:19; 11:22) The angelic glory-chariot escorted God first to the eastern entry, then out of the temple, and finally out of the city. The temple portal closed as God's glory departed Jerusalem carried upon the portable angelic chariot. That same glory appeared to Ezekiel in Babylon. *"I was among the captives by the river of Chebar, the heavens were opened, and I saw visions of God."* (Ez. 1:1)

If the glory moved to Babylon, one would expect to see the evidence that someone came under the influence of a heaven different than the ancient demonic one established by Nimrod, Babylon's chief architect and altar-builder. Although other examples may be found, an important illustration occurred in the life of Nebuchadnezzar.

Daniel 4:1-3: *"Nebuchadnezzar the king, unto all people, nations, and languages, that dwell in all the earth; Peace be multiplied unto you. I thought it good to shew the signs and wonders that the high God hath wrought toward me. How great are his signs! and how mighty are his wonders! His kingdom is an everlasting kingdom, and his dominion is from generation to generation."*

As was described in chapter six, altars have attendants in both realms. Man attends the earthly base and connects with a deity in the heavenly realm. Man's authority and the spirit's power converge at an altar to influence all that dwell in the sphere of authority of that priest and that supervising deity. Nebuchadnezzar came under the influence of God. Therefore, who was in Babylon raising an altar, attending that altar, opening a portal, and releasing the glory? One man functioning in that priestly capacity was Daniel.

Abstaining from the Influence

Daniel was among the sons of the kingly or princely seed lines of Judah that Nebuchadnezzar appointed to learn the language and knowledge of Babylon. The young men were brought unto a tutor and appointed daily food and wine from the king's provision. All this was to prepare them to stand before the king and serve him in his Babylonian court.

When the food was offered to Daniel and his friends Hananiah, Mishael, and Azariah, whose names were later changed to Shadrach, Meshach, and Abednego, the young men respectfully refused. The head of the eunuchs feared to grant Daniel his request, lest the boys looked malnourished and it was discovered that he disobeyed the king's order. Daniel asked for a ten-day trial, which was granted. At the end of the ten days, *"their countenances appeared fairer and fatter in flesh than all the children which did eat the portion of the king's meat."* (Dan. 1:15)

Why did Daniel not want to eat the king's meat? Why did he set his heart not to defile himself with the king's food? Certainly Daniel might have been schooled in the dietary laws given under the Mosaic covenant. Although, since most of Moses' spiritual and moral laws were disregarded prior to the deportation, Judah may not have been observing ceremonial, civil, or dietary laws either. Daniel's parents could have been among the faithful who remembered God's commands, observed the ordinances, and taught God's Word to their children. Daniel certainly demonstrated that he had knowledge of the ways of God. Therefore, Daniel could have declined based entirely upon his understanding of clean and unclean food.

Another spiritual principle, however, may have been at work in the scenario. Judah was not sent into captivity for disobedience over those things that defile the body but for those that defile the soul. Judah's practice of idol worship defiled the nation. Jesus added more light to the subject of defilement when he commented:

Matthew 15:16-20: *"And Jesus said, Are ye also yet without understanding? Do not ye yet understand, that whatsoever entereth in at the mouth goeth into the belly, and is cast out into the draught? But those things which proceed out of the mouth come forth from the heart; and they defile the man. For out of the heart proceed evil thoughts, murders, adulteries, fornications, thefts, false witness, blasphemies: These are the things which defile a man: but to eat with unwashen hands defileth not a man."*

Jesus taught that the heart, not the stomach, was the seat of defilement. Whatever a man allows to enter the heart defiles the heart and is expressed through words and actions. Likewise, Proverbs 4:23 warns a man to guard the heart with great diligence for it was the place from which all matters of life spring.

Idol worship contaminated the hearts of the citizens of Judah and was the cause of defilement. Therefore, the question arises as to whether or not the food offered to Daniel was in any way connected to idols. A story from the days of Jeroboam, Israel's first king in the Northern kingdom, sheds some light.

I Kings 13 records a time when a prophet from Judah came to Bethel, the spiritual capitol of the Northern Kingdom, where Jeroboam had erected a golden calf. The prophet found the king burning incense at an altar. He prophesied to the altar that a king of David's lineage would be born who would offer the false priests, both living and the bones of those who had died, upon the altar. To verify the word, the altar broke, spilling the ashes and coals to the ground. As Jeroboam heard the prophetic declaration, he reached his hand toward the altar. Immediately his hand dried up. The king asked the prophet to intercede on his behalf. At the prayer of the prophet, the king's hand was restored.

In gratitude, Jeroboam invited the prophet to his home for reward and food. The prophet declined stating that God had warned him not to eat any bread or drink any water while in Bethel. Because the prophet was called to overcome the altar, which would require the release of more spiritual power than that which the human agent and the supervising spirit were generating, he was warned to avoid coming under the influence of anything that may have been dedicated to the worship of that deity. If Jeroboam was tending the altar, his household, his food, his drinks, and his heirs were being consecrated to facilitate the agenda of the satanic force connected to the altar. God told the prophet not to eat or drink of those things that served as contact points for demonic authority. He was warned not to come under the influence of any token of Bethel's idol worship.

Later in the story, an older prophet heard of the happenings at Bethel, and he pursued the younger prophet to invite him to the old man's home. Why had God not sent the older prophet to speak to the altar? Why did God call a man from Judah to come to the spiritual center of Israel to release a word? Was there not a prophet in Bethel who qualified? Apparently, the older man was indeed a prophet; because Scripture defines him as such. However, God did not select him to release the judgment. The reason becomes clearer as the story continues.

Upon the invitation, the young prophet declined again stating that God had warned him not to eat any bread or drink any water in the land. The older prophet lied and said that an angel had given him the directive to bring the young man home for bread and water. The young man obliged, entered the prophet's home, ate and drank, and went on his way. As he returned to Judah, a lion came out and killed him. What caused the young prophet's death?

The bread and water of the older prophet might have just been a symbolic representation of the young man's obedience. Incomplete obedience might have been the cause of a punishment sent from God. That is possible. Another possibility rests in the nature of the bread and water. The prophet of God had probably not directly dedicated his household with its provision upon altars of false idol worship. However, the waters from which he drank were the earthly containers of the idolatrous vapors that ascended over the land. The bread that he ate grew from the ground under the management of the territory's prevailing spirit. The old man was not qualified to speak to the altar because he had become influenced by the spiritual climate of Bethel and was, at least metaphorically, a partaker of the tokens of the altar. His power was weakened. His word was tainted in that he lied. And, his bread and water were defiled.

By ingesting Bethel's bread and water, the prophet from Judah came under the influence of things that served as contact points for demonic authority. He defiled his consecration, not his belly. He compromised his sanctification. The power released through and the protection provided by his portal had become compromised. The lion, representing the kingly spirit over the land, gained the advantage over the prophet to unleash retaliation.

Turning attention back to Daniel, the young men refused the victuals dedicated to the king and the gods Nebuchadnezzar worshipped. Daniel set his heart not to be defiled. Daniel determined not to come under the influence of pagan altars. Daniel wanted no point of contact between his heart and a token of demonic consecration. Daniel made a deliberate choice to raise an altar and to vow his obedience to the God of his forefathers. Light dawned on a new day for Daniel in the land of his captors, and he made a decision as to the purity of the worship that he offered. It could be said that Daniel fulfilled the re-creation pattern of erecting a worship-tabernacle in his Babylonian heaven on his metaphoric day two.

Consecrating a Priest

Daniel's first test of his priestly ministry in the foreign land was a face-off with the magicians, astrologers, and wise men of Babylon. Moses had to test the power of his portal over that of the Egyptian sorcerers. Elijah had to demonstrate the authority of his portal over that of Baal's prophets. Daniel's time had come. Portals into the second heaven cannot prevail against portals into the throne of God. Was a gateway to the highest Heaven open over Daniel?

Nebuchadnezzar dreamed a disturbing dream; but when he awakened, he was unable to recall it. He called his wise men, but they were powerless to tell the dream and, thus, could offer no interpretation. They even defended their inability by declaring that there was not a man who could comply with such a request. The king would need a god to assist him. Nebuchadnezzar was so angry that he put out a decree that all wise men in Babylon should be killed.

When Daniel heard of the edict, Daniel appeared before the king and requested a temporary stay of the order to allow Daniel time to seek God and come again before the king with the interpretation. The petition was granted. Daniel and his friends prayed because they did not want to perish with the rest of the wise men of Babylon. Daniel tended his prayer altar. The Heaven opened and God downloaded a night vision and the understanding.

Daniel went again before the king and described a great image that represented the Babylonian kingdom and three kingdoms that would arise after Babylon's day of dominance. At the end of the fourth kingdom, God would set up His kingdom that would break in pieces and consume all others. The kingdom God would establish would stand forever. (Dan. 2:31-45) Nebuchadnezzar praised Daniel, acknowledged his God, and made him ruler over the whole province of Babylon. Unlike the Pharaoh of Moses' day or Ahab of Elijah's day, Nebuchadnezzar's heart responded without retaliation to the presence of God's glory.

Although the king promoted Daniel, he was yet not converted to the worship of Daniel's God. He erected a large image of gold and required that all fall down and worship the image when music was played. Daniel's friends did not bow to worship, which angered the king who sentenced them to be burned alive in a furnace. The fires of the king's rage were exemplified by his command to heat the blaze seven times hotter. The Hebrew men were cast inside the furnace. The portal, which was being serviced by the altar ministry of Daniel and his friends, surrounded them. The flames did not touch them. The fires of the god of Nebuchadnezzar failed to break into the fire that burns without consuming. That flame, which Moses had experienced upon Mt. Horeb, was engulfing Shadrach, Meshach, and Abednego in Babylon. And, as with the portal opened to Moses, so with Daniel's portal, God was present. Heaven connected and the king was allowed to view a fourth man, a Heavenly visitor, present in the portal.

The power of the portal was not a mystery to Nebuchadnezzar. He knew that the level of a sorcerer's power was in direct correlation to the level of consecration of that magician to the deity that empowered him. For more power, the wizard entered a higher level of dedication and became the contact point for a stronger demon. The same principle holds true in the black arts that are practiced today. The stronger the wizard, the stronger the demon. The more powerful the spirit, the higher the level of covenant enacted by the priest who services the altar of that spirit. Nebuchadnezzar knew how the spirit world functioned. Therefore, he spoke of the Hebrews:

Daniel 3:28: *"Then Nebuchadnezzar spake, and said, Blessed be the God of Shadrach, Meshach, and Abed-nego, who hath sent his angel, and delivered his servants that trusted in him, and have changed the king's word, and yielded their bodies, that they might not serve nor worship any god, except their own God."*

The young men had covenanted with God to the utmost. They offered the highest sacrifice of their own bodies. They refused service or worship to any other deity. They were single in allegiance, dedicated in duty, and faithful in commitment. They did not compromise their covenant, which released the non-compromising reciprocal Heavenly response.

A third contest was generated in which Daniel demonstrated his ability to resist the influence of an idol and those persons who served an evil agenda. During the reign of Darius, Daniel was set as the highest of three presidents who ruled over one hundred and twenty princes. His prominent position evoked retaliation. The other presidents sought occasion to set a snare for Daniel. They provoked the king to decree a law that no one should make a request of any god or man for a thirty-day period except for those made to King Darius. Anyone who defied the law was to be cast into a lion's den. Darius complied.

As was Daniel's custom, he went to his house and prayed to God three times a day. The conspirators reported Daniel's activities to Darius and reminded the king of the binding nature of the law of the Medes and Persians, which was that the king's words could not be revoked. Much to his dismay because of his love for Daniel, Darius ordered Daniel to the lion's den. Throughout the night, the king fretted; and early the next morning, the monarch came to the den to inquire if Daniel had been kept alive by his God. Daniel's voice responded from inside of the den: *"My God hath sent his angel, and hath shut the lions' mouths, that they have not hurt me: forasmuch as before him innocency was found in me; and also before thee, O king, have I done no hurt."* (Dan. 6:22)

Those who had sought Daniel's harm were cast to the lions and utterly destroyed. Daniel's portal had protected him from retaliation. He stated the reason. He was innocent before God and before the king. Sin was not found in him. The Devil could find no weak spot in the portal or no entry point to attack. Years earlier, a false prophet named Balaam had been hired to put a curse upon Israel so that the enemy of Israel, Balak, could harm them. Every time Balaam tried through sorcery to open a portal of power from the high places of Baal, he would connect with Israel's portal and Israel's God. God would not allow Balaam to curse Israel because there was no sin or idol worship that had created a point of entry. Proverbs 26:2 affirms that the curse will not attach without a cause. In Psalm 57, David declared his trust in the shadow of God's wings that protected him when his soul was in danger from Saul's armies, who he metaphorically called lions. David spoke that those who had set the trap for him would themselves fall into their own pit. Perhaps Daniel recounted the psalmist words while spending the night with the lions.

Throughout various levels of consecration, Daniel refused to defile himself with the things dedicated to devils, proved his superior power over the king's magicians, cast down the power of the golden image, and found shelter in the portal from spirits of retaliation. His power level and portal-opening ability was well tested. Daniel released Heaven into the earth.

Servicing the Altar

Evidence abounded that Daniel's prayers had the power to pierce the heaven in Babylon. A demonically structured heaven acts like a shield between the earth and the glory of God. When a portal into God's throne is opened, the shield is effectively penetrated. The presence, influence, power, and blessings that were previously locked up are released. For example, light came to Nebuchadnezzar; and he was converted. (Dan. 4:34-37) Daniel serviced his altar by prayer and non-compromising dedication.

Daniel was granted understanding of the word of Jeremiah, which decreed that Israel's captivity would only last for seventy years. (Dan. 9:2) Daniel began to confess the iniquity of his forefathers. He repented for the idolatry that had caused the captivity. He acknowledged the veracity of God's commandments. He affirmed the justice of God's actions. Finally, he sought God for forgiveness.

Daniel set his heart to repair the altars that Judah had neglected. His repentance was equivalent to canceling the leagues made with idols. His confession functioned to cast down false altars. His affirmation of God's Word and ways reinstated the covenant. Daniel was servicing the altar. He was offering the vapors of prayer and creating a cloud on his side of the firmament. While he was yet praying, Gabriel appeared through the portal to instruct Daniel about the future of Judah.

On another season, Daniel was fasting for twenty-one days and repenting for the sins of his nation. The Heavenly realm again became manifested through the portal. A Heavenly personage appeared and revealed that the demonic shield had taken twenty-one days to penetrate. Michael, one of the chief angels had assisted in a contest with the chief demon over Persia. Daniel had attended the altar at its earthly base until the angelic ladder was successfully open and Heaven could pierce the shield. Revelation of the future was again granted to Daniel along with the guarantee that the portal's supervising angels were warring as his heavenly counterpart to maintain the open portal.

The portal remained effective throughout the days of Judah's captivity. The last king that Daniel served was Cyrus, who was the man responsible for the decree to release the Jews to return to Jerusalem and who funded the rebuilding of the temple and the city.

II Chronicles 36:22-23: *"Now in the first year of Cyrus king of Persia-- in order to fulfill the word of the Lord by the mouth of Jeremiah-- the Lord stirred up the spirit of Cyrus king of Persia, so that he sent a proclamation throughout his kingdom, and also put it in writing, saying, 'Thus says Cyrus king of Persia, The Lord, the God of heaven, has given me all the kingdoms of the earth, and He has appointed me to build Him a house in Jerusalem, which is in Judah. Whoever there is among you of all His people, may the Lord his God be with him, and let him go up!'"* (NIV)

Into a rebuilt city and unto a restored people God sent His only Son at the season of the fourth world empire, just as Daniel had been told.

CHAPTER EIGHT

Heroes of Faith: The Empowerment to Release Heaven on Earth

Remembering the Faithful

Daniel was faithful in the courts of Heaven and in the courts of Babylon. What he heard in Heaven he spoke on earth. That which God allowed in Heaven, Daniel allowed on earth. That which God forbid in Heaven, Daniel rejected on earth. Daniel structured the heaven and the earth over which God had given him authority after God's pattern. Daniel was faithful.

Others were likewise faithful to Heaven's mandate in the days of captivity. Shadrach, Meshach, and Abednego, Daniel's friends, withstood the pressure of idol worship. Esther, the young Jewish maid became queen of

Persia and, along with her uncle Mordecai, protected the Jews from mass execution. Ezekiel recorded the words of the prophet to the exiles.

Before the death of Daniel, Cyrus made the decree to release the captives to return to Jerusalem and rebuild the waste places. Ezra and Nehemiah recounted the deeds of the faithful remnant who returned. Haggai, Zechariah, and Malachi were devoted prophets sent from God to His people in the days of restoration. Genealogies were provided that communicated priestly and kingly lines that had been preserved for God's purposes and His glory. Many were faithful.

God has always had His elect. God has always reserved a faithful people for Himself and for His plan. Recall that Elijah thought that he was the only one who remained that had not bowed to the altars of Baal. God reminded His righteous servant that there were seven thousand who were likewise faithful. Although not all the personal stories of all the loyal believers are recorded in detail throughout the pages of Scripture, untold numbers served God in their generations. And, all that lived for God comprise a great company of witnesses.

Hebrews 11 recalls the lives of the faithful: some by name, some by deeds, and many undifferentiated except that God commended them for their faithfulness. They lived by their faith in God and His immutable Word. They, like Daniel, only allowed on earth that which God allowed in Heaven. They, like Daniel, refused any structure of the heaven or the earth over which God had given them authority except that which matched Heaven's pattern. They all knew something that was first true in the unseen realm, and then endured every earthly contradiction to that Heavenly truth until the earth reflected Heaven's mandate. By faith, the saints of old obtained a good report.

Enjoying the Eternal

Out of nothing but God's Word came everything that exists. The church has long held as orthodoxy the doctrine of Ex Nihilo, which means that all things came into being from no other source than the Word of God. (Col. 1:16-17) Eternity came before time. God moved from His eternal, unseen realm to form the seen realm. II Corinthians 4:18 states: *"So we fix our eyes not on what is seen, but on what is unseen. For what is seen is temporary, but what is unseen is eternal."* (NIV) Two realms exist:

the seen and the unseen. Unseen was first. It was preeminent. It was the pattern. It was the prototype. All reality originates from the unseen.

Once the seen realm was structured, God created Adam and Eve and placed them in the earth to manage the temporal after the pattern of the eternal. They were to follow God's example and cultivate the physical to reflect the glories of the non-physical. Their heaven was to be God's throne and their earth was to be His footstool; in other words, God would reign from man's heaven and all His ways would be 'walked out' in the earth.

Adam and Eve had a great advantage in finding Heaven's pattern. They existed in communion with God, were surrounded by the reality of God's realm, and personally experienced Heaven on earth. Man and God walked and talked together in the garden. The garden was an earthly throne for God. His realm of glory surrounded Adam and Eve. They were clothed in glory and splendor just like God wraps Himself in light. (Ps. 104:1-2) They were not subject to death. Their dirt bodies, which were wrapped in glory, were fit for both Heaven and earth.

Although God had set the firmament to separate His Heaven from man's heaven, the realities of God's Heaven were overlaid upon the earth. There was no death, no lack, no pain, no sin. The firmament veil could be penetrated. God's realm was accessible to man and man's realm was accessible to God. Heaven and earth converged in the garden.

Into the garden came the serpent. The origin of the serpent was not from the eternal but from the temporal. Out of the serpent's mouth came another word that contradicted the Word of Heaven. The serpent challenged that the temporal should govern the eternal. The serpent indicated that the seen had more reality than the unseen. The serpent contested that the earthly needs should have dominion over the Heavenly mandate. Adam and Eve believed the lie. They prioritized the seen above the unseen.

By seeking to elevate the created above that which was without beginning, they unplugged from the truth, disconnected from the reality, and detached from the eternal. They plugged into a lie, connected with the counterfeit, and attached to the temporal. They went from being Heavenly creations who lived in the earth to being earthly creations bound to the earth. They fell from the realm of glory. Immediately, they noted that the light suit that surrounded them had disappeared. They were only earthly.

The firmament veil was no longer open for man to pass to God and God to pass to man. The veil closed, and the first couple were consigned an earthly dwelling outside of God's glory. Scripture revealed ways and seasons when portals opened and passage between the two realms became possible, but the open Heaven of Adam and Eve was altered by the sin in the garden.

Locating the Unseen

Before the fall, man had no trouble locating the realm of God. After the fall, Heaven became inaccessible. Heaven seemed far away. Because man was bound to a three-dimensional existence with a heart that was wicked (Jer. 17:9) and a mind that was alienated from God's wisdom (Rom. 8:7), Heaven had little impact in either providing a model for human activity or for releasing the glories of that realm to invade earthly existence.

The sphere or realm of Heaven often was considered the place where the righteous would live after they departed from earth by way of death. Although limited in definition, that concept is accurate. Adam's earth body lost its Heavenly covering. He and his heirs were no longer suited for dual realms. While Adam was on the earth, he lived in a body fashioned for his earthly connection. However, his earth body was destined to return back to the earth. Once that happened, he could no longer continue in the physical realm. Some part of the unseen realm then became his dwelling place.

However, Heaven is more than a far away destination waiting to house departed souls. Scripture often presents Heaven as interfacing with the earth but on a level beyond that which the five physical senses can detect. For example, recall the story of Elisha and his servant when the King of Syria was at war with Israel. (II Kin. 6:8-17) King Ben-hadad gathered with his officers and set his battle plans against Israel. God revealed the Syrian's plans to Elisha who informed the king of Israel of the schemes of their enemy. Ben-hadad thought that one of his own was a traitor who told the war plans to Israel, but his servants informed the king that the prophet in Israel was the cause of his trouble.

Ben-hadad sent horses, chariots, and a mighty army to encompass Dothan, the city where Elisha was dwelling. When the prophet's servant saw the strength of the enemy that had come against them, he responded in great alarm. Elisha told him not to be afraid for the army that was with them was greater than the army of Syria. At Elisha's request, God pulled back the veil for the servant to see into the spiritual realm. He saw the mountains full of horses and chariots of fire round the prophet.

Heaven had dispatched a host to protect and defend Elisha. From where did they come? Exactly where was the realm of Heaven? One theory has Heaven located a considerable physical distance from which God dispatches His messengers at light speed. That description reveals three-dimensional thinking. If something is not near and visible, it must be far and invisible. To become visible, a distance must be traveled to get from far to near. Because the realities of the material realm became predominant in Adam's fall, the previous explanation fits with a temporal definition of visible and invisible.

However, there is another explanation that is more in keeping with Scripture. The realm of Heaven is near, but in another dimension. Throughout normal physical life, man can interact with two or three dimensions plus time. However, Heaven is not accessible in any of those dimensions. In Adam, the veil was closed; but Elisha's servant got a glimpse into another sphere, another reality, another dimension. He saw not what had arrived from somewhere else, but what had been there yet was undetectable by his five senses.

Hebrews 12:1 says that believers on earth are compassed about with the cloud of witnesses comprised of those who have passed from the earth in death. The deceased saints are pictured as encircling or surrounding those alive on earth. The imagery of Hebrews 12 is the same as that of II Kings 6, the former encircling throng consisting of departed believers and the latter encompassing host made up of angels. Near but not here! Close but not detectable! Present but not visible!

In the last few decades of the 20th Century, science discovered the presence of extra dimensions. Known as Superstring Theory, physicists postulate that although the physical world exists in three dimensions plus time, at least ten or possibly more dimensions exist. Based upon theoretical and observational success, the String Theory is the proposal that the created order began from a point of origin. The Bible affirms that the entire created order began with God releasing His Word. The picture that emerges from these scientific findings is that the universe in its origin had spatial dimensions tightly curled up like a ball of string that began to uncurl in the initial creation event. However, at only 10^{-43} seconds after the cosmos began to expand, six of ten dimensions stopped uncurling while the remaining four dimensions continued to expand and became the observable universe known to man. Physicists believe that the non-visible six dimensions remain curled up at every location within the four dimensions of length, width, height, and time. Surrounding and at every level of the physical dimensions are strings of extra-dimensionality.

Before the technology of science could validate the unseen realm, the Bible unveiled it to those who had spiritual eyes to see. Ecclesiastes 3:11 says that God has set eternity into the hearts of men so that man can discover the works that God has done from beginning to the end. Eternity was set in man's heart as part of his original formation. He was created to fellowship eternally with God, function from eternal truth, and enjoy eternal bliss. If eternity were not invested inside of man, the unseen realm could not be knowable. But eternity, the realities of Heaven, the authenticity of another dimension, and the veracity of non-physical is knowable to man – especially the man of faith.

Operating by Faith

Hebrews 11 tells of people who saw into eternity and lived with a firm conviction that the unseen realm had preeminence over the seen. In essence, these people of faith lived like pre-fall 'adams.' They were eternal first and temporal last. The writer of Hebrews opens the dissertation about the cloud of witnesses by describing the characteristic that all the cited believers had in common. They all were commended for their faith.

Hebrews 11:1-3: *"Now faith is the substance of things hoped for, the evidence of things not seen. For by it the elders obtained a good report. Through faith we understand that the worlds were framed by the word of God, so that things which are seen were not made of things which do appear."*

Their faith not only acknowledged an unseen realm, but stood assured that things locked up in the unseen realm were meant to be released into the seen realm. Their faith realized that those hoped-for, unseen realities originated beyond the temporal realm. Because *"the things which are seen were not made of things which do appear,"* their faith understood how the seen realm came into being. Seen things came from unseen. The unseen was first. There was a vehicle that released the realities of the eternal to create the physical. God's Word was the vehicle. God's Word laid out the heavenly pattern. God's Word released Heavenly realities in the earth. Heaven was causative. Heaven was the primary.

The Hebrews 11 cloud of witnesses acted just like God acted. They believed that which was true in Heaven's realm and then acted upon that basis of reality. They aligned their actions and words to harmonize with the actualities of Heaven. Adam and Eve failed the faith test. They doubted that those promises of God, which were as yet unseen, had essence, content, and substance. They became earth-focused. If they couldn't see it, it wasn't reliable. Conversely, the saints of Hebrews 11 were commended because they believed the invisible and acted accordingly.

Hebrews 11 recalls the faith deeds. Abel offered the substitute blood sacrifice that released Heaven's forgiveness upon the sons of men. Enoch spent his days peering into the unseen realm and received the revelation of God's plans for redemptive history that covered the ages until the end of time. (Jude 1:14) Noah saw the coming flood and acted correspondingly in the earth by building a boat. Abraham heard the promise of a seed line and trusted that he and Sarah, too old to conceive, would produce a child. Patriarchs passed God's covenant down through the family lines because they believed the land promised to Abraham would be their land. Joseph died in Egypt but commanded his sons to take his bones with them when God sent them to possess the covenant land. Moses refused the reward of Egypt because he believed the invisible promises of Abraham to be greater than the physical reward that Pharaoh could offer. Moses saw the invisible King.

Because the faith heroes peered into Heaven, reached into Heaven, and believed for Heaven to be released in the earth, supernatural power was available to them. They conquered kingdoms, administered justice, gained what was promised, stopped lion's mouths, escaped furnaces of fire, were rescued from the sword of the enemy, and prevailed valiantly in battle. Others chose death rather than giving up their testimony of the reality of the eternal realm when tortured, mocked, scourged, imprisoned, stoned, or slain by the sword. These all held fast that the eternal was of greater value, had more lasting significance, and was based upon a more enduring nature than the temporal or earthly.

The truth of the unseen was comprehended by and lived out through those who comprised the cloud of witnesses. The dimension of Heaven was not only the basis for what they thought, it was the reason behind their deeds. They lived to bring Heaven to earth. And when Heaven was released upon the earth, properties from another reality and laws from a different dimension superceded physical laws. Miracles happened.

Releasing the Miraculous

Operating in three dimensions plus time limits what is possible to the laws of physics. God establishes His laws. God is not a man that He changes His mind. His laws are steadfast. He created all things by His Word and then maintains His creation by that same powerful Word. (Col. 1:16-17) When a miracle occurs, it appears that the laws of nature are temporarily suspended so God can do something out of the ordinary. Suspending His laws would be in contradiction to His person and His Word. However, by considering the concept of dimensions, both the steadfastness of natural laws and the possibilities of supernatural occurrences merge without contradiction.

The dimension of Heaven operates in laws not limited to gravity, electromagnetic fields, and strong and weak nuclear forces, which are principles that govern the earth. Heaven was first and is the greater. Earth and the physical realm were created from and answer to the greater. The day will come when the eternal will swallow up the temporal with all its limitations, including its physics. Because of the higher laws of Heaven, when Heaven's dimension engulfs or opens to the earth, other laws supercede physical laws. This intervention is called a miracle.

Places where Heaven and earth connect are portals. Not only do Heavenly beings come to earth through portals, Heaven's laws prevail on earth at portals. Human agents serve altars by faith, which is by believing that the power and presence of Heaven can and will invade the earth. Dimensions converge at a portal that is opened by faith. When dimensions converge, miracles are released.

Consider the miracle of Joshua as he fought with the five kings to dispossess them from Canaan. (Josh. 10) As Joshua led the children of Israel to inherit the land, the fear of God's people began to spread to those who occupied Canaan. They had crossed the Jordan River by an event not dissimilar to Moses and the Red Sea. The water stopped flowing to allow the nation to cross over and then resumed its flow after the people passed. Waters are not inclined to stop and start unless something blocked and then released the flow upstream. Allowing for a natural explanation like something or someone damming up the waters affords a possible, although not probable, physical explanation for the event. Whether one accredits the crossing to miraculous intervention of the heavenly dimension or extraordinary manipulation of ordinary circumstances, the occupying nations heard of Israel's crossing.

Shortly afterward, the Israelites fought against Jericho. They marched, shouted, and blew trumpets. The enormously wide and tall fortress of exterior walls fell straight into the ground. Again, allowing for a natural explanation like an earthquake affords a possible, although not probable, physical explanation for the event. Again, whether one accredits the falling walls to miraculous intervention of the Heavenly dimension or extraordinary manipulation of ordinary circumstances, the occupying nations heard of Jericho's defeat.

Five kings conspired together to fight with the Gibeonites, who out of fear for their lives had made a league to serve the Israelites. Gibeon called to Joshua for help and the Israelites went up to battle. Israel prevailed and began to chase the Amorite kings. God sent great hailstones from heaven and killed more by the hail than Joshua killed by the sword. Again the question may arise: miraculous intervention of the Heavenly dimension or extraordinary manipulation of ordinary circumstances? However, the next event removes all questions.

Joshua 10:12-14: *"Then spake Joshua to the Lord in the day when the Lord delivered up the Amorites before the children of Israel, and he said in the sight of Israel, Sun, stand thou still upon Gibeon; and thou, Moon, in the valley of Ajalon. And the sun stood still, and the moon stayed, until the people had avenged themselves upon their enemies. Is not this written in the book of Jasher? So the sun stood still in the midst of heaven, and hasted not to go down about a whole day. And there was no day like that before it or after it, that the Lord hearkened unto the voice of a man: for the Lord fought for Israel."*

That day in battle, Joshua saw by faith the unseen realm and reached into another dimension. No matter how many possible natural explanations are superimposed upon the previous 'miracles,' there can be no doubt about the sun and moon standing still. Without contradiction, that day a portal was opened. Laws from a higher dimension were imposed. By natural law, the earth would have had to cease to rotate, suspending gravitational forces and causing things to fly into space. Or, the sun and the moon would have had to change their orbits to remain in the same placement in the sky as the earth continued to orbit. That explanation is equally impossible as the timing of the heavenly bodies is precisely fixed in all the celestial 'clocks.' What happened? A higher dimension with higher laws opened over Joshua, and a Heavenly phenomenon was experienced as an earthly miracle.

The heroes of faith lived by the conviction that the greater truth had a Heavenly origin. However, their conviction was not philosophical in nature. It was practical. What they knew to be true in the Heaven motivated the words they spoke and the actions they took. They lived to conform the earth to Heavenly patterns. Faith saw; faith acted; faith apprehended; faith released. Faith reached one hand into the unseen and set the other hand upon the seen. Faith stood in the gap until the two realms converged. When they converged, miracles occurred and Heaven restructured the earth.

CHAPTER NINE

Jesus: The Commission to Restructure the Heaven

Stewarding the Land

God created Adam and set him as steward over all the earth. God, Himself, owned both the Heaven and the earth. He created it; He had proprietary rights, ownership rights, landlord rights. God selected mankind to be the managers of His property. Adam was to work with the land and make it fruitful. Adam was to watch over the property to subdue any influences that were not in harmony with God's Heavenly patterns. Adam was granted kingly authority to make decisions for the earth. Adam, and all of humanity represented in Adam, was given a land lease.

When Adam turned his allegiance away from God to the serpent, Adam sold out to the Devil. One cannot sell what one does not possess. Adam was given a lease to the earth, which he legally transferred to the hands of the enemy. That act not only entrenched satanic powers in man's heaven, it also granted satanic powers legal rights in the earth. The Devil became the earth's manager. Scripture confirms this by referring to Satan as the god of this world (Jn. 14:30) and the chief ruler in the second heaven. (Eph. 2:2; 6:12)

Although able, God would not simply revoke Adam and Satan's right to steward the earth. God established His ordinances, and He lives to uphold His Word. The Heaven and the earth are founded on everlasting precepts and principles. (Ps. 119:89-91, 160) God, Himself, stands behind His Word to perform it. (Heb. 6:13-18) Therefore, to retrieve the land from unrighteous rule and to give it into the hands of a faithful steward was the goal; but the pathway required a legal transaction.

God began by appointing replacement 'adams' who could regain the title deed to the earth. From Noah's righteous son Shem came the patriarch Abraham. Abraham recognized God to be El Elyon, which means the Most High God who possesses Heaven and earth. (Gen. 14:19, 22) Abraham acknowledged God's priority rights over the earth. The owner is more important than the steward. Abraham accepted God's ownership of both the Heaven and the earth. When invited to enter covenant with El Elyon, Abraham accepted.

The cutting of covenant provided Abraham with provision from and protection by a higher authority than the god who was holding the land lease. Abraham built altars that opened portals that had the ability to break through the demonically-structured heaven and release God's hand of blessing. Abraham had abundant wealth. He was visited by angelic beings and protected from powerful kings. God's portal was at work over the patriarch and his family.

God promised to give Abraham a land grant. However, Abraham did not receive the land during his lifetime. Scripture clearly states that Abraham was a stranger in a foreign country, that he lived in tents, and that he sojourned throughout the land of Canaan. His son Isaac and grandson Jacob were heirs with Abraham of God's promise. They did not receive the land either. (Heb. 11:9) They were all granted a promise, but they did not occupy the land. The land remained under the stewardship of the seed line of Ham, Noah's unrighteous son who worked for the god of this world.

As biblical history unfolded, Abraham's heirs moved to Egypt, which was occupied by more of Ham's ancestry. They settled in camps of Goshen, which were lands owned by the Egyptians. Rather than land stewards, Abraham's heirs became slaves working the land for the god of Egypt, the god of Ham, the god who controlled the earth. As their oppression became unbearable, they cried out to God who sent Moses to deliver them. As has been previously discussed, Moses' rod had the power to open a portal into the highest Heaven, thus releasing God's power and presence throughout the land of Egypt. The god of Ham was being challenged. Satanic power over the heaven and the earth was proven inferior to that of the Most High God, Possessor of Heaven and earth. Moses' tenth and final miracle released the death of the firstborn.

God established an eternal principle when He gave the earth to Adam. The principle defined that the firstborn of a father was granted the birthright, which means stewardship of a father's earthly possessions. The law of the firstborn delineated that the right to rule passed from father to the oldest son in the family line. As the Heavenly

Father's firstborn, Adam was the heir of the birthright, the earth. When Adam sold out, he lost his right to rule for God. Satan took possession of the inheritance and began appointing sons who would manage the earth for him. World systems and earthly management passed from a satanic steward to the son of a satanic steward as the principle of firstborn rights was in operation in the earth.

However, the firstborn principle had a clause. All firstborn sons were to be set aside as holy before the Lord. (Ex. 13:2, 12; 22:29) Even as God set aside Adam to be holy for His service, so all firstborns were to have the same requirement placed upon them. That clause in the firstborn principle communicated that the heir apparent was not to be consecrated to serve any god other than El Elyon. Based upon biblical patterns, when the first of a thing is dedicated, the whole is considered holy. That same logic is inherent in the tithe and the firstfruit offering. By the clause that required the dedication of each firstborn, God could effectively restart a new holy seed line at any time the oldest son was consecrated.

Although Adam was originally consecrated, he sinned. The penalty for Adam's sin was mandated, which was death. Shedding of blood fulfills the death sentence.

God will accept the blood of a substitute as payment for the incurred death sentence. Upon payment of the penalty, God releases a pardon. No longer under God's judgment and justice, man returns to a holy or right standing before the Lord. Therefore, after Adam, a firstborn needed a blood atonement to be consecrated.

God had called Abraham into a covenant with Him. Abraham dedicated himself and followed God. Abraham was granted a son, Isaac. God commanded Abraham to offer Isaac as a sacrifice. What was God doing? God was operating the law of firstborn. God had promised a land grant to Abraham, but the oldest son must be consecrated before the inheritance could be transferred. Abraham obeyed and took Isaac to Mt. Moriah. There, God revealed a substitute ram that Abraham could use as an atoning offering. Because Abraham consecrated his only son of promise, he secured the land grant for his heirs.

In Egypt, God enacted His clause of redeeming and consecrating the firstborn. Because all men or animals that opened the matrix were to be consecrated to God and because God would accept a blood atonement from an appropriate substitute, God instructed Moses to take the blood of a Passover Lamb and place the blood upon the door posts of each home. The applied blood was to testify that the firstborn in that home was redeemed and was qualified to inherit a birthright. The Israelites obeyed the eternal precept. The Egyptians, however, did not accept the Passover Lamb. That night, a firstborn or the firstborn's substitute was offered unto God. No sons died of the Israelites. All eldest sons and firstborn animals died of the Egyptians, including the heir of Pharaoh.

Passover rescued condemned sons. Passover legally freed the firstborn from the need to die for his own transgression. Passover guaranteed that upon the death of a substitute, the firstborn of every home was redeemed and consecrated. By dedicating the first of every family, all the rest of Israel was representatively made holy unto the Lord. God announced that the Passover would be a new start for the nation. The firstborn principle had made them a holy people unto God. The whole nation passed from under Adam's death sentence and from under the tyrannical land management of the god of Ham, the god who held the land grant. The Most High God had consecrated a nation of firstborn sons, and He would give them the land grant that had been promised to Abraham.

Because Passover marked a new beginning, they were told to restart their calendar and make Passover the beginning of their year. They were told to celebrate it every year. A nation of consecrated sons departed Egypt with the spoils, which was evidence of their new status as inheritors. They were granted a new heaven in the cloud by day and the fire by night. They were guaranteed the right to occupy Canaan.

When the nation was ready to possess their land under the leadership of Joshua, they performed two covenant acts. They circumcised all the males, which was the visual sign God had given to Abraham as the seal of his covenant with El Elyon. Next, they celebrated the Passover, thereby consecrating again the firstborn of each family and thereby representatively declaring that the whole nation was dedicated to manage the earth for God. Under Joshua, the sons of Abraham triumphed over the sons of Ham as they dispossessed the Canaanites. Although the entirety of heaven and the fullness of the earth were not transferred into their stewardship, a section of the earth was legally redeemed and restored to God's firstborn representative sons.

Throughout Israel's history, the covenant Abraham made with El Elyon and the land grant given at Passover were effective, as long as Israel upheld their end of the covenant terms. However, when Israel broke covenant, they compromised the portal that had been opened through the demonically-structured heaven into God's Heaven. Without Heaven's protection, enemies invaded attempting to repossess the land. When Israel repented, God released divine help to reclaim the land. Eventually, they, like Adam of old, dedicated their 'eden' to the serpent. They forfeited firstborn rights, were disqualified as land stewards, were expelled from the land of promise, and sold into captivity. Without redeemed firstborn sons, the earth's lease remained in the hands of the god of this world. God set about to appoint another replacement 'adam' who could regain the title deed to the earth.

Appointing a Qualified Heir

God had set the requirement - only a qualified firstborn could inherit the land. All of Adam's heirs, including the cloud of witnesses, could only be eligible when the blood of a substitute paid the redemption price. No one could buy back any more of the land than they had the spiritual collateral to fund. All the replacement 'adams' lacked Adam's original level of authority, as he was appointed steward of the whole earth. Therefore, in the fullness of time, God sent to earth His only begotten son, Jesus, whom Scripture declares to be the Last Adam. (I Cor. 15:45)

Adam was the first created son; Jesus was the only begotten son. Adam was made from the earth; Jesus was sent from Heaven. Adam was given an earthly body that housed the Spirit of God; Jesus was the Spirit of God that took on an earthly suit. Jesus' authority to inherit the birthright was not only equal to Adam's; it was superior. Satan was aware that God had promised a seed who would demolish the serpent's headship and reclaim the land grant of the earth. (Gen. 3:15) Mistaken that Moses was the promised heir, Satan prompted the destruction of Israelite sons through Pharaoh, whose act of murder sealed his own doom years later. At the birth of Christ, Satan again prompted the death of Jewish sons through Herod. Satan knew he must defeat the firstborn to maintain his land grant.

Jesus was sent to restore what the first Adam forfeited. His earthly ministry was inaugurated at His water baptism. The Heaven opened, the Holy Spirit moved into man's heaven in the form of a dove, and God's voice was heard to announce *"Thou art my beloved son, in thee I am well pleased."* (Lk. 3:22) The Spirit and the Word were released from Heaven. Again, a metaphoric day one dawned upon the earth. God initiated a new day and appointed a new heir. God testified that Jesus was His son who was chosen to manage. What would Jesus do on His day two?

Immediately after His baptism, Jesus was taken by the Spirit into the wilderness where, after forty days of fasting, He was tempted by the Devil. The parallel of His temptation with that in the garden is undeniable. Eve was tempted to look at the fruit and see that it was good for food. In Jesus' first temptation, Satan wanted Him to look at a rock that could become bread. Jesus responded that whatever portion God's Word provided for Him would be the only food that He would eat. He would not listen to the word of another god to secure earthly sustenance.

Secondly, the Devil caused Eve to doubt the veracity of the promised spiritual inheritance. He suggested she should eat and become like god. If she believed this other god's pathway to heavenly power and followed his word, she would ascertain spiritual blessings. Similarly, Satan suggested to Jesus that He should jump from a high place. If Jesus followed his suggestion and believed his word, Jesus would discover His level of spiritual power. The angels would come to His rescue. Jesus responded from Deuteronomy 6:16 that following the word of another god to open a portal into the spiritual dimension would provoke the jealous anger of God. Jesus would only follow God's pathway to spiritual authority and power.

Finally, the Devil caused Eve to eat. She took the inheritance that the serpent offered. She gave more worth to the enemy than to God. She and Adam worshipped the Devil and transferred their earthly management authority into his hands. Correspondingly, Satan took Jesus to a high mountain and showed Him all the kingdoms of the world. Satan promised to give Jesus the kingdoms in exchange for His worship. One cannot sell what one does not own. The god of this world, who was granted earthly authority through Adam and Eve, was seeking to disqualify a potential heir. If Jesus came to reclaim the earth grant, then He could have it from Satan for the small price of worship. Would He take the inheritance the Devil offered? What would Jesus do on His metaphoric day two? Would He worship Satan and fortify the demonic-firmament? Would He submit His position as an heir to a serpent? Jesus responded, *"Get thee hence, Satan: for it is written, Thou shalt worship the Lord thy God, and him only shalt thou serve."* (Mt. 4:10)

Jesus passed the test that Adam and Eve failed. On His day two He erected a worship-firmament. Qualified as an heir by birth order and by obedience, Jesus went forth under an open Heaven to build Heaven into the earth.

Establishing a Gate

Jesus went throughout Judea and Galilee releasing the power and presence of Heaven. He was restructuring the earth to reflect the righteousness and the freedom found in God's realm. If Jesus was channeling Heaven's power, He was living under the influence of a portal. That portal was identified in a conversation with one of His disciples.

Philip, who had been called by Jesus to follow Him, went to find his brother Nathanael. Philip convinced his brother that Jesus was the prophet about whom Moses had written (Deut. 18:15-19) and urged Nathanael to go along with him to meet the Lord. As Nathanael approached

Jesus, the Lord spoke that He had seen the brother of Philip as he sat under the fig tree. Nathanael responded to the fact that Jesus possessed that supernatural knowledge by declaring, *"Rabbi, thou art the Son of God; thou art the King of Israel."* (Jn. 1:49)

Jesus told Nathanael that he had only begun to see things that would stir his faith. How would he respond if he saw Heaven open and the angels of God ascending and descending upon the Son of man? (Jn. 1:51) Jesus' comment was undoubtedly a reference to Jacob's ladder. Jacob, who had come under the authority of Abraham's portal opened at Bethel, had seen a ladder through which Heaven was released. When Jacob came under the influence of the portal, he responded by saying that God was there and he had not even recognized His divine presence. Jesus was letting Nathanael know that the portal was present to influence. Nathanael had come under the power of the open Heaven, and he responded with a covenant response of belief, just as Jacob had done years before.

Furthermore, Jesus was communicating that He was the Ladder that came from Heaven. He had not only come to identify a gateway to Heaven; but He, Himself, provided the bridge whereby Heaven connected to earth and earth joined with Heaven. Heaven would traffic to earth and earth would climb to Heaven on Jacob's Ladder, now identified as Jesus.

Jesus was Jacob's Ladder; Jesus was the portal. The evidence of an open Heaven was found in all His deeds. He multiplied the fish and loaves. Such a miracle confirmed that the laws of another dimension were superceding earthly laws. He walked on water. Physical laws prohibit such activity, but when properties of another dimension merged with the earth, even Peter could stand upon liquid. Apparently, without faith, Peter was not able to abide in the portal. When he stepped out of the Heavenly dimension, the physical properties of water caused him to sink. (Mt. 14:25-31)

Jesus' connection to the highest Heaven was demonstrated by His authority to cast out devils, whose power was located in a spiritual dimension lower than God's Heaven. The influence of His portal caused many to believe and follow Him. He also demonstrated authority over the effects of the fall by healing diseases, restoring physical bodies, and even raising the dead. Jesus' portal was so effectual that it provided Him a place of safety from all human or demonic retaliations. (Lk. 4:28-30; Jn. 19:10-11)

Erecting the Firmament-Tabernacle

Jesus faithfully attended His altar. He would spend His early morning hours in a solitary place in prayer. (Mk. 1:35) The imagery of the Altar of Incense emerges. Jesus lifted up His prayers under His firmament-tabernacle. He constructed a cloud on His side of the firmament upon which the presence of God would ride. Jesus structured His heaven after the pattern of God's Heaven, and God took a seat in Jesus' clouds. Everywhere He walked, He carried the glory upon His shoulders. (The imagery of the cloud is clearly explained in chapter five.)

The Jews had a tradition that communicated a man's responsibility to become a walking carrier of God's glory. Moses commanded the men of Israel to fasten tassels of twisted cords to the four corners of the outer garment as a reminder of God's laws and the Israelite's covenant obligation to God's Word. (Num. 15:38-39; Deut. 22:12) These twisted coils traditionally were the fringe on a prayer shawl, which the men would put upon their heads at prayer time. After prayer, the shawl was draped over the shoulder and worn as a sign of piety. Jesus condemned the practice of the Pharisees who made their tassels extra long just to make a religious show before the people. (Mt. 23:5) Although He condemned the abuse, the Lord obeyed the command of Moses by using and wearing the shawl.

As a man lifted the shawl over his head during a season of prayer, the man was erecting the symbol of a canopy. In Moses' day, only the Levites could enter inside the Tabernacle; but all Israelites could tent with God under their shawls. There, inside the canopy, the man of God would pray. Symbolically, the prayer would send up the vapors of incense and create a cloud inside the shawl tent. That which transpired inside the Tabernacle had its corresponding action inside the individual's tent. God moved His glory into the cloud that was created by the incense. In essence, each believer was afforded a means to open a portal through prayer that would then rest upon his shoulders as he walked throughout the day.

Elijah had such a prayer shawl, which Scripture called his mantle. His successor, Elisha, wanted the mantle of Elijah. Elisha was certainly speaking about the spirit and power that was upon his father, but he was also asking for the prayer shawl. The prayer canopy of the prophet was saturated with the glory cloud. The prayer shawl was an earthly house of Heavenly glory. When Elijah was taken up, the mantle floated back to the earth. Elisha picked up the prayer shawl, struck the water, and cried, *"Where is the Lord God of Elijah?"* (II Kin. 2:14) The water parted. The portal opened by the former prophet remained open for the latter prophet because of the prayer shawl.

The practice of prayer shawls continued to Jesus' day. Each morning, Jesus tabernacled with God. Throughout the day, the glory resided with Him, in Him, and upon Him. One day a woman who had suffered for twelve years with a blood condition pressed through the crowds to reach Jesus. (Mk. 5:24-34) She determined to touch the hem or fringe on His garment. The word used in the Greek is *kraspedon,* which means twisted coils. She wanted to touch the edge of His prayer shawl. When she did, her condition was immediately healed. Jesus perceived that power had been released as she touched the fringe. She reached into the portal. She knew that the fringe was like the edge of the glory tent. If she could even get to the edge, the glory of Heaven, which was housed in Jesus' tabernacle, would reverse the curse of her condition. She was correct. The prayer canopy of Jesus was saturated with the glory cloud. His prayer shawl was an earthly house of Heavenly glory.

Jesus lived in two dimensions. The barrier that Adam had erected between man's heaven and God's Heaven did not restrict His movement between the two realms. He communed with God. He spoke what He heard the Father say. He did those acts which He saw His father do. He was never banished from God's presence as Adam and all his progeny had been. John testified: *"The Word became flesh and made his dwelling among us. We have seen his glory, the glory of the One and Only, who came from the Father, full of grace and truth."* (Jn. 1:14, NIV) Heaven tabernacled in earth through Christ Jesus.

Opening the Heaven

With only two exceptions, all portals that were opened required an altar consecrated by blood. Adam's original altar was the first exception. God placed him under an open Heaven. Not until he sinned was his heaven closed. His heirs could not approach God without the payment required of Adam for his transgression. Adam was placed under a death sentence. The placing of blood upon the altar was evidence that the penalty had been paid.

Once justice was satisfied, man and God could meet at a blood-stained altar.

Jesus' portal was the other exception to the requirement of blood to consecrate an altar. Jesus was without sin. He had not inherited the sin or the penalty from Adam. Jesus did not need to provide blood as evidence that His sins were covered; He was sinless. His Heaven was open. Everywhere He walked, He was the point of convergence of Heaven and earth.

Jesus maintained His open Heaven. His earthly ministry provided for others the benefits of His portal. Jesus enforced the superior power of Heaven over all the earthly works of the enemy. He modeled for humanity how an 'adam' should live. Never before Him had a man so successfully structured his heaven and his earth in conformity to Heaven's pattern. However, Jesus came as the Last Adam to destroy all the work of the Devil. (I Jn. 3:8) Because Adam placed humanity under a death sentence and gave the earth to the stewardship of the god of this world, Jesus was sent to undo all that Adam had done. The death penalty and the land grant were not dealt with in His life; these two reversals could only be accomplished by His death.

John the Baptist called Jesus the Lamb of God who came to take away the sin of the world. (Jn 1:29) John described the purpose of Christ's coming to earth. He came to finalize the payment for the death sentence that Adam had incurred. All the years of substitute sacrifices had not fully cancelled the debt. The blood of animals was not equal payment for the blood of a firstborn son. To fully release a pardon over mankind, God required payment in full. All replacement 'adams' had arrived in the earth under an inherited sentence of death. Not until Christ came was there a replacement 'adam' without a hereditary debt. Jesus was a spotless firstborn whose blood had the power to atone for the sin of God's first son and all mankind that were represented in Adam.

Jesus went to Calvary. There He died to atone for the sins of mankind. God laid upon Christ the penalty due Adam and his heirs.

Hebrews 10:4, 5, 14, 17: *"It is impossible for the blood of bulls and goats to take away sins. Therefore, when Christ came into the world, he said: . . . "Here I am, I have come to do your will." . . . By one sacrifice he has made perfect forever those who are being made holy. . . . Then he adds,*

"Their sins and lawless acts I will remember no more." (NIV)

A Son for a son, a Firstborn for a firstborn, a Representative head of a new humanity for a representative head of an old humanity, a Last Adam for a first Adam – Jesus shed His blood and the sin debt was once-and-for-all covered. "It is done," was His cry from Calvary. "It is done," was the Father's echo from Heaven. Then He surrendered His life. Man and God were restored and reconnected at the blood-stained altar of Calvary.

The firmament-barrier that Adam erected through his disobedience had been substantiated through his expulsion from the garden. Angels were set at Eden's gate to guard the way so that man was not readmitted into God's throne. That closed gate represented the sealed-off, firmament-barrier. Later when Moses built the Tabernacle, he set a closed veil with embroidered cherubim between the Holy Place and the Holy of Holies. The veil of Moses, the gate at the garden, and the firmament-barrier all told the same story: Adam had caused mankind to be denied access to God.

On the day of Christ's atoning sacrifice, a miracle occurred in the Jewish temple in Jerusalem, which was a redesign and a reconstruction of Moses' Tabernacle. The veil that sealed off the Holy of Holies was rent. (Mt. 27:51) God was testifying! Moses' veil was open. Adam's gate was open. The way into God's throne was open. The Last Adam opened the sealed-up Heavens. Man was being invited to return to God's glory.

Jesus died, was buried, and arose from the grave on the third day. Death could not hold Him. Death's penalty had been nullified; therefore, death's power had been abolished. His resurrection verified that the death penalty was once-and-for-all cancelled. For the next forty days, Jesus appeared to His disciples in His glorified body. How could that occur? The dimension of Heaven was overlaying the earth. Jesus had a body suited to live in Heaven yet adaptable but not limited to the properties of the earth.

At the end of forty days, He ascended to Heaven on the cloud-chariot as His disciples watched. (Acts 1:9-11) His ascension was His bodily passing from earth to Heaven. He took an earth suit with Him. When Jesus came from Heaven, He was given a body in Mary's womb.

When He returned, He returned not just as the Lord of Heaven but as the Last Adam. In Christ, mankind was readmitted to God's Throne. When He sat upon the Throne, those who are 'in Christ,' or His 'body' of believers, were likewise granted a seat in Heaven. Listen to the scripture:

Ephesians 2:5-6: *"Even when we were dead in sins, hath quickened us together with Christ, (by grace ye are saved;) And hath raised us up together, and made us sit together in heavenly places in Christ Jesus."*

The Last Adam opened to man what the first Adam closed. Christ's own were forgiven, reconnected, and readmitted. Jesus was Jacob's Ladder upon whom Heaven came to earth and through whom earth returned to Heaven.

Reclaiming the Earth

Jesus died on Passover. God predetermined the day of His substitutionary sacrifice; it occurred on Passover. (Mk. 14:12-30) Jesus was the Passover Lamb. (I Cor. 5:7) If Jesus qualified to be the substitutionary sacrifice for Passover, then He must have fulfilled the principle of firstborn. Recall the statute. All firstborn sons were to be set aside as holy before the Lord based upon a blood atonement. And, when the firstborn of a seed line was consecrated, the whole family was representatively made holy.

Under Moses, the blood of the Passover Lamb rescued and consecrated all the firstborn sons throughout the dwellings of the Israelites. In Christ, God was again activating His law of firstborn. Jesus qualified to be the spotless, Passover Lamb. He was the first begotten of the Father as well as the firstborn of Mary and Joseph. He was qualified to provide an appropriate substitute.

Once the blood of the Passover lamb was applied, the firstborn was consecrated. He was holy. His lineage was holy. The whole family line was set aside as God's heirs, and the inheritance could be legally transferred. The blood of Christ began a new nation of consecrated heirs. Unconsecrated firstborns do not qualify for management. Unconsecrated firstborns do not qualify to receive the inheritance. Unconsecrated firstborns do not get the land grant. They are disinherited and dispossessed.

Once God finds a qualified firstborn race, He can recall the land grant from the false heirs and restore it to the true heirs. Jesus was a consecrated firstborn; and through His sacrifice, He consecrated a new blood line of heirs. He is God's heir and His people are joint-heirs. (Rom. 8:17) God recalled the land grant from the god of this world and gave it to His Son.

Psalm 2:7-12: *"I will proclaim the decree of the Lord: He said to me, "You are my Son; today I have become your Father. Ask of me, and I will make the nations your ineritance, the ends of the earth your possession. You will rule them with an iron scepter; you will dash them to pieces like pottery." Therefore, you kings, be wise; be warned, you rulers of the earth. Serve the Lord with fear and rejoice with trembling. Kiss the Son, lest he be angry and you be destroyed in your way, for his wrath can flare up in a moment. Blessed are all who take refuge in him."* (NIV)

The first Adam gave the land grant to the serpent. The Last Adam defeated satanic rulers to reclaim the land grant and give the earth into the hands of godly management. (Col. 2:15) The kingdoms, which the Devil offered to give Christ during the wilderness temptation, were reclaimed by El Elyon and reappointed to the legal heir. Jesus took a seat upon a throne in Heaven to rule all nations as the legal heir and steward of man's heaven and all the earth.

From His exalted position with all authority in Heaven and in earth (Mt. 28:18), Jesus sent the Holy Spirit into the earth. On the day of Pentecost, a portal opened over Jesus' church. The power of Heaven was poured out upon the disciples. They became the conduit, the gateway, the channel, the portal. At the top of Jacob's Ladder sat the enthroned Last Adam and at the base of Jacob's Ladder was the new Bethel, the new house of God. The Heaven opened and the church was commissioned to go into all the reclaimed earth to manage the inheritance. Christ had made man's heaven new and the coming of the Holy Spirit had made the earth new. Jesus had completely reversed the damage done by Adam. A new redeemed race was empowered to steward heaven and earth.

CHAPTER TEN

Believers: The Charge to Steward the Heaven and the Earth

Learning From the Pattern

The ministry of Moses and many of the works that he did can be paralleled in Christ. Moses was born to be a deliverer; so was Jesus. The Devil tried to eliminate both men through mass genocide when they were babies. Both were called of God to go to a people oppressed and enslaved by the god of this world. Both supernaturally challenged and defeated satanic rulership to provide freedom for the people of God.

Moses started the Passover; Jesus fulfilled it. Moses called out a blood-bought, consecrated nation to serve God. Jesus consecrated the new nation through His own blood that they might serve God. Moses and the Israelites departed Egypt under a new heaven created by a fiery pillar. Jesus sent His disciples out under a new heaven created by the presence of the Holy Ghost, who descended on the day of Pentecost as tongues (or pillars) of fire creating a new heaven for the church.

Moses built the Tabernacle, which served as an earthly open portal to Heaven. Jesus built His Tabernacle (I Cor. 3:16; I Pet. 2:5), which served as an earthly open portal to Heaven. Moses set a priesthood to tend the portal. Jesus appointed a priesthood to tend the portal. (I Pet. 2:5; Rev. 5:10) Moses brought Israel to the Promised Land and commissioned them to occupy and to steward the earth. Jesus pointed out the Promised Land for His church. *"And he said unto them, Go ye into all the world, and preach the gospel to every creature."* (Mk. 16:15)

The followers of Moses were given a land but not a free pass. The Promised Land was occupied with *"Hittites, and the Girgashites, and the Amorites, and the Canaanites, and the Perizzites, and the Hivites, and the Jebusites, seven nations greater and mightier than thou."* (Deut. 7:1) Israel had to dispossess the occupants of their promised territory. God would be with them. (Deut. 31:6) Their portal would open supernatural power. But, they had a job to do. They went to war. They defeated and ousted just enough enemies to bestow territories on all the tribes. Then they settled down and began to coexist with the inhabitants of the land. Their dominion was less than comprehensive. Their occupation was never finalized. God's command was less than fully obeyed.

The disciples of Jesus were given the whole earth as a promised inheritance. Similar to Moses, a land grant was not the same thing as a free pass. The earth was occupied. From Jerusalem to Judea to Samaria to the uttermost parts of the earth, the land was possessed with peoples and religions that were mighty and well-entrenched. Jesus promised to never leave or forsake His church. (Heb. 13:5) The portal opened by the Spirit would make supernatural power available. (Acts 1:8) But, a job must be done. And Jesus – He sits ruling from His throne until His church successfully makes every enemy His footstool. (Acts 2:35; Heb. 1:13; 10:13) Jesus will only be satisfied when every knee bows and ever tongue confesses that He is Lord. (Rom. 14:11) From Pentecost until today, the church has been mandated to spread His dominion over the whole earth.

Building the Altars of the Lord

Before Moses took the sons of Israel into the land to war, he built the Tabernacle and established its altars. He likewise consecrated the priests that were called to tend the altars. Canaan was filled with satanic altars and demonically-empowered priests that serviced the altars. Moses made sure that Israel's priests were well instructed in tending altars, because Israel would need to release more power than that which was being released from the counterfeit altars. Each battle needed to be won in the unseen realm before it could be won in the seen realm. Consecrated priests and altars secured the open portal and the release of Heavenly power.

According to the re-creation pattern, light dawns on day one. Once the call, the commission, the revelation, or the mandate bursts upon a man or a nation, the response must be altar-building. Day two sets up the altar, consecrates the priest and the altar, raises up the firmament-tabernacle, and secures man's heaven for a habitation of God's holy presence. After that, the earth is ready to be changed.

Jesus was the Light of the world that brought illumination upon the plan of God. His light not only shined to show people the pathway back to God, it also shined to show the saints the pathway from God into the nations of the world. God's dominion mandate came to light in Christ. The church went to altar-building, a day-two activity. They waited in the upper room until the new temple and the new priesthood was ready to receive Heaven's consecration. The oil of Heaven was poured out at the Pentecostal portal, and the new priests were ready to engage their demonic counterparts in all the world. They were ready for day three.

Building an altar and consecrating oneself at that altar is, therefore, the first priority of the commissioned. Abraham, Isaac, Jacob, Moses, Elijah, and all the heroes of faith were altar-builders. Consider the story of Gideon. (Jud. 6-8) The Midianites were oppressing the Israelites, stealing their crops, and impoverishing God's people. When Israel lifted a cry for deliverance, God sent an angel to visit a man named Gideon. The angel brought the light. Gideon had been selected to lead the nation to defeat their foe. Gideon needed a little proof that the angel was indeed a messenger from the Heavenly dimension, therefore Gideon requested a sign.

Gideon prepared a meal, which included a young goat, cakes, and about one half bushel of flour. The offering was plentiful considering the lack of bounty in the land. If the visitor had eaten the meal, Gideon would have had no verification of the supernatural. However, the visitor had Gideon place the victuals upon a rock over which he stretched his rod. Fire burst forth out of the rock and consumed the offering. At that, the angel vanished. Undoubtedly, a portal was present as the properties of fire, smoke, a rod, and a Heavenly being were all manifested.

Convinced of the light that just dawned, Gideon built an altar and called it Jehovah-Shalom, meaning covenant God of peace. Because God had arrested him to defeat the Midianites in order to return peace to Israel, Gideon erected an altar to the God of Peace. By erecting the altar, Gideon was doing two important things. First, he was opening a portal for the power of God to be released. Secondly, he was consecrating himself by bringing himself under the influence of the altar. Recall the definition of an altar. An altar is a place of spiritual power that is attended by an earthly priesthood who draws strength from the spirit that supervises the altar. Conversely, an altar is a place of spiritual power that is supervised by a spirit that releases other-worldly agendas through the altar's earthly priesthood. God needed an altar-tender – Gideon. Gideon needed the altar's power – God. That day of altar raising was a day of covenant.

Believers must build and tend altars of worship and prayer, altars of dedication and consecration, altars of reverence and obedience. The power level of one day may be insufficient for the battle that looms on the horizon. The strength to overcome a household enemy might not be enough strength to overcome a ruling spirit over a territory. The revelation of a former day may not sustain one's faith for a new day. Seasons of seeking God through prayer and fasting can open new dimensions of the believer's faith and power.

One day a man brought his son who had seizures to Jesus to be healed and delivered. The father had asked the disciples for help, but they were unable to cast out the demon and heal the boy. Jesus' response was rather revealing. He called the generation perverse and faithless. By perverse, Jesus was saying that they were headed in the wrong direction. By faithless, He was indicating that they were not persuaded of the purpose and power of that unseen realm. Jesus delivered and healed the boy. When the disciples inquired as to their impotency, Jesus told them that to overpower that level of spirit, they would need to fast and pray.

Fasting and praying are priestly functions that occur at altars. Jesus indicated that they needed to turn from whatever was occupying them and turn to an altar. Jesus admonished them that faith comes by hearing the Word of God, becoming knowledgeable of Heavenly wonders, and knowing the God they were serving: all of which are available revelations at an altar. In essence, Jesus called them to an altar in order to receive a heightened level of consecration and the subsequent release of power.

There are many of 'this kind comes out by prayer and fasting' battles that need to be fought as the church takes occupation of the redeemed earth. Many enemies, not unlike the Midianites, will only be routed out when a Gideon spirit rests upon the believer. A Gideon spirit is not a magic wand. A Gideon spirit falls upon a called, consecrated, altar-builder who makes a covenant of service with Jehovah-shalom.

Tearing Down False Altars

The same night that Gideon built the altar, God spoke further commands. Gideon was to tear down the altar to Baal erected by his father and destroy the Ashtoreth grove next to the altar. Gideon's father, Joash, also tended an altar. He serviced the altar of a demon god, and a high-ranking one at that. Gideon was sent to destroy the portal of satanic power. Gideon took ten men, went by night, cast down the altar, and cut down the grove.

An altar is the place where the spiritual world is accessed and released into the earth. To restrict demonic influence over the people and over the land, the portal to the second heaven must be closed. Those portals must be identified. The devil counterfeits the ways of God; therefore, any place or thing where God had chosen to manifest His Heaven is often found to have a counterpart in the kingdom of darkness. Altars are often found on mountains. God met with His people on mountains, cut covenants on mountains, and built His tabernacles on mountains because mountains represent ladders to heavens. (See chapter four.) Therefore, satanic portals are found in high places, both natural elevations and man-made mounts.

Stylized mountains such as pyramids, pillars, obelisks, and stones can be sites of demonic openings.

Groves and trees are also sites where portals are opened. Moses used a tree to open a portal. Moses' rod was a wooden stick, most likely a hewn tree branch. His rod could be called a stylized tree. In nature, trees stand between heaven and earth drawing the life from the earthly-based root system and also drawing vital forces from the air through its many branches. Trees are like channels for life to flow between that which is above and that which is below. God was communicating to Moses that his deliverer's tree branch would act as a conduit or conductor between Heaven and earth. The rod of Moses became a movable portal, releasing the Heavenly dimension into the earth. The magician's or sorcerer's wand is the satanic counterpart.

Throughout Scripture, trees symbolize kingdoms and God's people are compared to trees. (Ps. 1:3; 92:12) Like a tree, kingdoms are rooted in the earth but spread their influence into the heavens. God used the tree analogy for Nebuchadnezzar, and then told the king that he would be cut down. (Dan. 4) Because God's people and God's kingdom are compared to trees, the enemy will use trees and tree stumps as contact points to establish his kingdom on the earth. His first use of the tree was the tree of knowledge of good and evil found in Eden. The prophets spoke of idol worship occurring at trees. (Is. 57:5; Jer. 2:20; 3:6)

Other points of contact can be anything consecrated or dedicated to a demon god. Jacob commanded his family to give to him *all the strange gods that were in their hands and all their earrings that were in their ears.* Paul's preaching at Ephesus resulted in those who practiced magic destroying their articles of sorcery. (Acts 19:18-19) God's power was manifested through Elijah's mantle, Jesus' prayer shawl, Paul's handkerchief, and anointing oil. However, God's power is released by faith and not through magical artifacts and formulas.

Waterways are also sites for the release of demon spirits. Moses dealt with the waters of Egypt in the first three plagues, thus contesting with demonic strongholds. Elisha broke a curse carried on the waters by casting salt into the waters. (II Kin. 2:20-21) Moses cast a tree into the bitter waters of Marah and they were healed. (Ex. 15:23-25)

When possible, demonic altars and artifacts should be destroyed. When a public monument, a mountain, or a river is the source of an altar, the covenant made at that spot can be cancelled by repentance and declarations of God's Word over the site. One generation can and must repent for the sins of a previous generation. Daniel identified with the sins committed by Israel. He fasted and repented for many days. His intercession for the false altars that Israel had erected was arduous and extensive. For Daniel, destroying the ancient altars was not without a high price; but it yielded very high benefits. Likewise, Gideon took responsibility for the altar that his father had erected. He tore it down and he built a new one upon which he sacrificed one of his father's young bullocks. His repentance wasn't costless either, but his act reversed the effects of the altar and freed the land from the enemy's oppression.

Defeating the Enemies of God

Once Gideon closed the negative portal and opened God's portal, the battle began. The men of the city arose in the morning to find the altar torn down, the grove destroyed, and a bullock sacrificed on the new altar. They wanted to know who had done the deed, so they inquired. Because the city was asleep when Gideon accomplished his nighttime raid, there could only be two sources of information. One of the ten accomplices could have told or could have confided in someone else who gave out the information. Another possibility remains. An inquiry could have been made to satanic powers through some priest of Baal skilled in occult practices. Certainly the supervising spirit of the destroyed altar had knowledge of Gideon's activity.

The book of Acts tells of a time when seven sons of a Jewish priest named Sceva tried to cast devils out of a man in the name of Jesus whom Paul preached. The evil spirit answered from the man and stated, *"Jesus I know, and Paul I know; but who are you?"* (Acts 19:15) Jesus' name and power was known throughout the demonic realm. Paul had likewise earned a reputation in the satanic hierarchy. However that information network is constructed, knowledge of Paul's deeds and power had been disseminated. Likewise, Gideon's name had become infamous in the unseen realm. The supervising spirit leaked his name and stirred retaliation.

The men of the city were ready to kill Gideon. They demanded that his father, Joash deliver the young man unto them. Joash responded that if Baal was truly god, he could defend himself and could plead his own case against Gideon. These men did not need to defend Baal. Joash even changed Gideon's name to Jerubbaal, which means 'let Baal plead.' Apparently, the portal that was opened at the altar of Jehovah-Shalom was effectively at work providing protection from the retaliation. God granted peace from the vengeance of the citizens, and Gideon went forward to rout out the Midianites.

Reflecting back to the story of Elijah and his contest against the prophets of Baal, a contrast can be observed between Elijah and Gideon. Both successfully tore down an altar. Both came under a spirit of retaliation. Jezebel was furious with Elijah and swore his death within a day. Elijah fled from the wicked queen and the spiritual powers she used to execute her witchcraft. He did not go forward to rout out all the other altars throughout the land, cut down all the groves, and confront the enemy of Ahab and Jezebel.

Scripture is silent as to whether this was an error on Elijah's part or if he had accomplished all that God had mandated for him to do. He, like Gideon, found a portal of protection from the spirits of retaliation. However, Scripture does indicate that he, like Gideon, would need to finish what he had started. God told Elijah to appoint Elisha, Jehu, and Hazael who would complete the contest against the ruling king and queen. Believers who tear down altars will incur the retaliation of the supervising spirit of the altar. Having begun the process, the saints of God must finish the battle by routing the enemy from the land.

God gave Gideon a plan to attack the camps of Midian. His numbers were weak – only 300; his weapons were implausible – pitchers, lamps, and trumpets; but his help from Heaven was marvelous – the enemy soldiers turned on each other. When Gideon did arrived at the Midianite camp, the confused host fled and Gideon's band pursued. Messengers were sent and reinforcements came to Gideon's aid until the war was won.

In the days of Gideon, throughout Israel's occupation of Canaan, or in the advancement of Christ's kingdom into all the earth, the battles against the enemies of God are fought by people. Gideon fought against and destroyed real people, as did the Israelites when they occupied Canaan. Believers are not called to war against flesh and blood, but against spiritual enemies. (Eph. 6:12) God's eternal intention was that His wisdom would be demonstrated to rulers and authorities in heavenly realms through His people. Adam failed to reveal the superior ways of God in his contest with the serpent. Jesus, the Last Adam, superbly made known the flawless and matchless wisdom of God. That assignment was transferred to the church. The saints are to unveil and show forth the excellency of God's eternal will before the rulers in the heavenly domains. (Deut. 4:5-8; Eph. 3:10)

God gave the church a Gideon-like plan to attack the camps of the enemy. At times of weakness, the Scripture admonishes *"be strong in the Lord, and in the power of his might."* (Eph. 6:10) When the weapons seem implausible, the Bible informs that *"the weapons of our warfare are not carnal, but mighty through God to the pulling down of strong holds."* (II Cor. 10:4) And as it was for Gideon so it is for the church – God's help from Heaven is available. Heaven stands ready to release power through an altar that is dedicated to His name.

Believers are warned to war effectively by knowing the wiles of the enemy and by wearing the armor that has been provided.

Ephesians 6:10-17: *"Finally, my brethren, be strong in the Lord, and in the power of his might. Put on the whole armour of God, that ye may be able to stand against the wiles of the devil. For we wrestle not against flesh and blood, but against principalities, against powers, against the rulers of the darkness of this world, against spiritual wickedness in high places. Wherefore take unto you the whole armour of God, that ye may be able to withstand in the evil day, and having done all, to stand. Stand therefore, having your loins girt about with truth, and having on the breastplate of righteousness; And your feet shod with the preparation of the gospel of peace; Above all, taking the shield of faith, wherewith ye shall be able to quench all the fiery darts of the wicked. And take the helmet of salvation, and the sword of the Spirit, which is the word of God."*

Satan has wiles, which is the word *methodeia* in the Greek, which means the methods or tricks that he uses to entrap or ensnare. (Eph. 4:14) The spiritual armor covers several vital areas of the believer. A helmet represents a mind that is renewed by God's Word rather than being so spiritually childlike that it is open for every suggestion thrown by satanic subtlety. (Eph. 4:14) The girdle wraps itself around the loins, which is the hip or procreative region and suggests that the Christian should not only have the head knowledge of truth but should be able to reproduce truth in the daily walk.

The breastplate covers the vital organs of the heart and lungs. All the believer's spiritual affections and life energies should be established by the redemptive work of salvation. No heart attachments, no lustful longings, no unsanctified passions can flow from the heart or be breathed out as strange incense. The footwear is the gospel. God told Joshua that everywhere he walked he could dominate the land for his occupation. The believer is to advance the kingdom through the proclamation of God's Word, which is the sword of the Spirit, as the church moves out into every land formerly occupied by an enemy of God.

Finally, faith acts as a shield to quench all retaliation. Recalling from chapter eight, faith releases in the earthly realm that which is locked up in the spiritual realm. Faith manifests the unseen. Faith evidences the dimension of Heaven. All fiery darts from the second heaven cannot burn when one is surrounded by the fire that doesn't consume. Remember Shadrach, Meshach, and

Abednego? Satanic fiery darts lose power when faith has opened a portal to the throne of God.

The warfare of the church is not about kicking people out of a job, an inheritance, or a home. The church's battle is not accomplished by hurling bombs or slinging slander. The heirs of Christ are to war in the heaven. Moses rearranged Egypt's heaven. He battled. He spoke God's declarations into the earth, and God confirmed His Word with signs. Moses contested with spiritual forces until the demonically-structured heaven was dismantled. The earth then showed visible signs that the enemies in the second heaven had been disordered and confounded. The Israelites were set free.

Paul said, *"the god of this world hath blinded the minds of them which believe not, lest the light of the glorious gospel of Christ, who is the image of God, should shine unto them."* (II Cor. 4:4) As man's heaven is conquered, eyes will be open that were formerly blinded. Gideon saw the evidence of new eyes. His father, Joash, was the priest who serviced the altar of Baal. But when Baal's altar was dismantled and God's altar was erected, the blinders came off the old man's eyes. He defended his son, acknowledged the superiority of the God of his son, and put a challenge before his god to put up or shut up.

Jesus said, *"No man can enter into a strong man's house, and spoil his goods, except he will first bind the strong man; and then he will spoil his house."* (Mk. 3:27) The battle occurs in heaven and the results are demonstrated in the earth. To dispossess an enemy in the earth, the believer must first bind the controlling demonic stronghold that rules from man's heaven. Once the strongman is bound, the reclaiming of the earth, its inhabitants, and its resources will follow.

Binding the power of the strongman may require diligence and perseverance. It may also require insight as to the legal hold by which the spirit claims authority. Sins, perversions, occult activity, bloodshed, vows, and broken covenants serve as legal ground that provide an unseen fortress from which the enemy holds his grounds. Repentance for sins, denouncing vows and occult covenants, and offering restoration where possible severs all official claims for enemy occupation. Once all legal doors are shut, the enemy can be routed and the land can begin to cooperate with a new Heavenly arrangement.

When man's heaven is the dwelling place of God's Spirit, the land and the people rejoice.

Restoring the Land

Gideon defeated the Midianites and brought peace to the land. The Israelites wanted to make him and his heirs their kings. Gideon refused. He stated, *"I will not rule over you, neither shall my son rule over you: the Lord shall rule over you."* (Jud. 8:23) Scripture communicates that the land was in peace and quietness for the next forty years. The effects of Gideon's altar that had been dedicated to Jehovah-Shalom had influence over the land and over the inhabitants. The land, the fields, and the people prospered. Gideon, himself, had seventy sons and many wives and died at an old age.

As has been well documented, Adam and humanity, representatively, were given the earth to manage. When Adam fell, the earth reflected his fall. He altered the structure of his heaven and the earth testified to the perverted heaven. The earth yielded a perverted crop – thorns and thistles.

All that God made in the first six days of His creation was established on His Word. The created order was founded upon Heaven's ordinances. The creation communicates and obeys God's embedded Word. For example, God told Noah that the bow would remain in the sky to speak of a covenant that God made with creation. He would not destroy it again by flood. Psalm 19 tells that the heaven is inscribed with God's glory and that it declares His story. The psalm continues to state that the firmament shows His handiwork, meaning that the heavenly bodies that are visible in man's skies make known the craftsmanship of the Creator. The creation testifies all day, all night, and in all parts of the earth. An accurate Word is bound in the creation; an ordinance is firmly established in nature; and God's Law governs the created order. Romans 1 confirms the reliability of creation's testimony to not only communicate to mankind but to also provide an accurate legal witness by which man will be judged.

The ordinances of God must be followed. Man's side of the firmament-heaven must be structured as a habitation for God's glory. God's ordinances bind the heaven to obey His Word. Man's earth must be structured according to God's commandments. God's laws created the earth and were fastened to it. Moses required that the Israelites harmonize the witness of heaven and the earth.

(Deut. 4:6; 30:19) Moses called the heaven and the earth to testify either for or against its managers. If the managers followed God's everlasting Word, the heaven and the earth should agree and respond with blessing. If the managers changed the ordinances and broke the covenant, the heaven and the earth would rebel. (Is. 24:5-6; Deut. 27; 28)

When earth managers continue to abusively structure man's heaven and earth contrary to God's set regulations, the earth and heaven begin to communicate ineffective management. Crops fail, pestilence occurs, too little or too much rain falls, disease increases, and crime escalates. Heaven and earth are talking. They are testifying against the managers. Eventually, creation rejects, revolts against, or 'vomits out' the inhabitants. The heaven and the earth, which are bound to God's creation ordinances, shake. Earth kicks out its rulers. Heaven shakes and disturbs the satanic structures. God doesn't allow unbroken or continuing management from non-consecrated firstborns. He promised that they would be cut off in the third or fourth generation. (Ex. 20:5) Illegitimate towers to the heavens, like the one at Babel, will be frustrated. No long-term attempt to pervert the creation ordinances will be successful. When the shaking ends, God sets sanctified heirs with firstborn rights into place to manage the heaven and the earth. (Ps. 37)

Romans 8:19-22 states that the creation is groaning like a woman in labor to be delivered into the full efficiency that is locked up in its womb. That release is tied up with the earth managers. As the mature heirs begin to release God's mandates under the firmament and order earthly structures by those same mandates, the earth will cooperate and yield fruitfulness and blessing. Adam subjected the creation to bondage and the creation eagerly awaits sons of the Last Adam to liberate it from that bondage.

Believers have the mandate to reconcile all things in heaven and earth back to God's original creation ordinances. This is possible because the blood that Jesus shed removed Adam's curse and reconnected all things back to God. Believers are given the directive to make peace in heaven and in earth through that blood. (Col. 1:19-20)

If the church will do as Gideon did and tear down false idols, raise godly altars, and rout out the enemy, then the land will yield the peace that Jehovah-Shalom released in Gideon's day. However, the blessing released through

Gideon did not continue after his death. Gideon made a mistake that sacrificed the peace in the next generation.

Maintaining the Victories

The story of Gideon doesn't close with a happy-ever-after ending. Although Gideon rejected the offer of a hereditary monarchy, he asked that every man give him the golden earrings taken from their conquests. Gideon melted down the gold and cast it into the image of a priestly ephod, which he put on display in the town of Ophrah. This was apparently bad judgment because the end result was that, *"all Israel went a whoring after it: which thing became a snare unto Gideon, and to his house."* (Jud. 8:27)

Gideon corrupted the altar that had benefited him and all of Israel. God had given an altar where Gideon had made a covenant with Jehovah-Shalom. There is no mention in Scripture of Gideon maintaining that altar. The altar had functioned as a portal to release the power and presence of Heaven. If the altar was maintained or used, the Scripture is silent. However, the Bible does say that Gideon set up another place of commemoration and adoration. He built a golden ephod.

An ephod was part of the priest's garment that Moses instructed to be made for the sons of Aaron. Made of linen, the ephod had two sections, one covered the chest and the other covered the back. The sections were joined at the shoulders by golden rings and onyx stones upon which were engraved the names of the twelve tribes of Israel. Attached to the front of the ephod was the breastplate. Inside the breastplate were placed two stones called the urim and thummin, which were objects used by the priests in determining the will of God.

Gideon's ephod indicated that he was assuming a priestly role although he was not of Levitical descent and thus not qualified for such service. Secondly, the golden ephod most likely functioned as some form of a consulting device to gain secret knowledge for the unseen realm, a counterfeit of the urim and thummin. This is suggested because the nation went after the ephod in whoredom, which is a term used repeatedly of Israel when the nation followed idolatrous practices. Later in Judges 17, a man named Micah appeared who made an ephod and a teraphim, which is a term applied to an image used for divination purposes. Micah was following a practice that was acceptable at that time, which probably began with Gideon.

The golden ephod was set in the city of Ophrah. God had set His Tabernacle and priesthood in Shiloh in those days. There is no indication that God had consecrated another tabernacle, another priesthood, different priestly garments, or another city. Gideon offered metaphoric strange incense, which God had forbidden. Although the Bible does not speak to Gideon's intentions, it does clearly communicate his actions. His old day merged with his new. He had syncretism, or a mixture of two religions. He attempted to worship God with old pagan practices. Like Israel who possessed the land but did not finalize the occupation, Gideon placed a snare before his family and before his nation. Abimelek, Gideon's son whose name means my father is king – a title that Gideon had feigned to decline – led the nation into the snare that Gideon had laid.

Consecrated altars become key sites for the attack of the Devil. He delights in desecrating the holy. If he can pollute an altar, he can close a portal. If he can close portals into God's Heaven, then his portals into man's heaven can be more effective. Consider the portal at

Bethel, which was opened by Abraham and attended by Jacob. The Ark of the Covenant was kept in Bethel under the care of Phinehas, the grandson of Aaron. (Jud. 20:26-28) Samuel held court in Bethel and dispensed justice from the city whose name meant House of God. However, when the nation divided, Jeroboam set Bethel as one of the seats of golden calf worship. (I Kin. 12:28-13:3) One of Israel's chief portals was closed. The nature of the city became so changed under the influence of another altar and a demonic portal that the prophet Hosea called it in contempt Beth-aven, which means the house of idols. Only after Israel's capture and deportation by the Assyrians was there any reclaiming of Bethel. King Josiah, the final righteous king of Judah, tore down all the false idols within his own land and then went into Bethel where he uprooted every vestige of idol worhip. (II Kin. 23:15-20)

Mt. Moriah stands out in biblical history for its altars. Abraham offered Issac to God on Mt. Moriah. (Gen. 22) The power of the covenant made between the patriarch and Jehovah-Jireh, the God who provides a sacrifice, was so effective that years later the portal had the power to stay God's hand of judgment. II Samuel 24 recounts that David sinned by numbering the people. The consequence was a plague that spread over the nation. Scripture describes an angel with an extended sword passing over the land until the angel came to stand at Araunah's threshing floor, which was located on Moriah. God called the angel to stop. The portal that was opened by Abraham was still testifying that God would provide a sacrifice. God instructed David to go up and raise an altar. David was sent to reengage the covenant made between God and Abraham and to fortify the altar. David bought the land and the sacrifice. He built an altar. The plague was stayed.

Mt. Moriah became the site upon which the Temple of Solomon was erected. The sanctified mountain became the resting place of the Ark and the opening of a portal from Heaven. On the dedication day, the Heaven opened over the Temple and the presence of glory was so strong that no one could even stand for the weight of God's glory released through the portal. (I Kin. 8:1-11)

As Solomon's kingdom prospered, he married many wives who were not from Israel. As he intermarried with women from pagan countries, his wives brought their idol worship and corrupted the altars in Israel. The altar on Mt. Moriah was a chief target of satanic corruption. Solomon built high places for other gods and the subsequent kings converted Solomon's Temple into a house of demons. Satan's target was and is the consecrated altars. Close the altar; change the heaven. Change the heaven; control the earth.

Moses required a yearly covenant renewal. Passover was to be kept every year. Aaron was ordered to consecrate the Tabernacle, its vessels, and its priests with blood every year on the Day of Atonement. Each generation of priests required the same dedication ceremony that was demanded of Aaron. Covenant renewal maintains the altar.

The believer is called to covenant renewal at the communion table. Partaking of the elements reconnects, rejoins, reunites the Christian with the body and the blood, which efficaciously opened the portal to Heaven and by which the believer was consecrated. To attend the altar of communion without proper heart consecration and life dedication is to defile the altar. Paul warns that the effect will be sickness rather than healing, death rather than life. Properly maintained communion altars keep open a portal of power and protection. Paul warns the Corinthian church not to be ignorant of the altar's power. (I Cor. 11:23-32)

To properly service an altar, a priest must identify and consecrate the next generation. Abraham trained up his sons and taught them to build and worship at altars. Moses set aside the whole Aaronic lineage to be priests and the Levites to be those who would service the tabernacle. Elijah anointed Elisha to follow in his footsteps. Jesus empowered the church. Paul imparted to his spiritual son, Timothy. That which is gained in one generation can be forfeited in the succeeding generation, if the importance of altar-tending is not taught and if the next generation is not sanctified.

The secret of the portal is not to remain hidden. Each generation should train up the next to love the courts of God and to attend unto the altars of God. In Psalm 84, the psalmist declared that the altars were to him as a nest was to a bird. Even as the bird laid her eggs and raised her young from her nests, so were the altars of God to the man whose heart was after God. They were home. They were a resting place. They were generational.

Some would seek to open a portal for the power. In this, they are not unlike the satanic priests. Some would seek to open a portal for the miracles. In this, they are not unlike the witchdoctors. Some would seek to open a portal for the protection. In this, they are not unlike the sorcerers. But those men whose hearts are set on the courts of God will seek to open a portal for the Presence.

When righteous men open portals to Heaven, the glory of eternity floods into the earth. Eyes are opened to truth. Lives are freed from oppression. Hearts are converted for eternity. When godly men open portals to Heaven, the power of righteousness prevails upon the earth. Justice is released. Love is experienced. Mercy triumphs. When holy men open portals to Heaven, the realities locked away from humanity become accessible in the earth. God is glorified. Christ is exalted. The whole of creation is set free to worship.

May the church of Jesus step into the ministry
of opening portals into glory!

BIBLIOGRAPHY

Amsden, Patti. *The Law of Boundaries*. Kirkwood, MO: Impact Christian Books, Inc., 1999.

Bako, Abu. *Establishing God's Altar Everywhere: Taking the High Places*. Ghana: Heartland Publications, 2004.

_____. *Praying Through the Gates of Time*. Nigeria: Rehoboth Publishing, 2005.

Bolz, Shawn. *The Throne Room Company*. North Sutton, New Hampshire: Streams Publishing House, 2004.

Brown, Rebecca, M.D. *He Came to Set the Captives Free*. New Kensington, PA: Whitaker House, 1986.

Cho, Paul Y. with R. Whitney Manzano. *Prayer: Key to Revival*. Waco, TX: Word Books Publisher, 1984.

Dawson, John. *Taking Our Cities for God: How to Break Spiritual Strongholds*. Lake Mary, FL: Creation House, 1989.

Engle, Lou with Catherine Paine. *Digging the Wells of Revival*. Shippensburg, PA: Revival Press (an imprint of Destiny Image Publishers, Inc.), 1988.

Hagan, Robert. "Redeeming the Land" audio series. St. Louis: Prepare the Way Ministries, 2002.

Illustria Media. "The Case for a Creator" video presentation. Illustria Media, 2006.

_____. "Unlocking the Mystery of Life" video presentation. Illustria Media, 2002.

Jackson, John Paul. "Heavenly Portals & Protocol: Untapped Gateways to God" audio series. North Sutton, NH: Streams Ministries International, 2006.

Jacobs, Cindy. *Possessing the Gates of the Enemy.* Grand Rapids: Chosen Books, 1991.

_____. *The Voice of God.* Ventura, CA: Regal Books, 1995.

Johnson, Bill. *When Heaven Invades Earth: A Practical Guide to a Life of Miracles.* Shippensburg, PA: Treasure House (an imprint of Destiny Image Publishers, Inc.), 2003.

Jordan, James B. *Through New Eyes: Developing a Biblical Worldview.* Brentwood, TN: Wolgemuth & Hyatt Publishers, Inc., 1988.

Kimuli, Michael. *Effective Fervent Prayer.* Chichester, United Kingdom: New Wine Press, 2002.

Malone, Dr. Henry. *Portals to Cleansing.* Irving, TX: Vision Life Publications, 2002, 3rd printing 2005.

Myers, John. *Voices From the Edge of Eternity*. Old Tappan, New Jersey: Spire Books, 1968.

Newport, John P. *Demons, Demons, Demons: A Christian Guide Through the Murky Maze of the Occult*. Nashville, TN: Broadman Press, 1972.

Peters, Ben. *Signs and Wonders: To Seek or Not to Seek*. Fairfax, VA: Xulon Press, 2002.

Ross, Hugh. *Beyond the Cosmos*. Colorado Springs: Navpress, 1996.

Sheets, Dutch. *Intercessory Prayer: How God Can Use Your Prayers to Move Heaven and Earth*. Ventura, CA: Regal Books, 1996.

Silvoso, Ed. *That None Should Perish: How to Reach Entire Cities for Christ Through Prayer Evangelism*. Ventura, CA: Regal Books, 1994.

Strong, James. *The New Strong's Exhaustive Concordance of the Bible*. Nashville: Thomas Nelson Publishers, 1990.

Swenson, Richard A., M.D. *More Than Meets the Eye: Fascinating Glimpses of God's Power and Design*. Colorado Springs: Navpress, 2000.

Tenney, Tommy. *The God Chasers*. Shippensburg, PA: Destiny Image Publishers, Inc., 1998.

Thayer, Joseph Henry. *A Greek-English Lexicon of the New Testament.* Grand Rapids: Baker Book House, 1977.

Towns, Elmer L. *Praying the Lord's Prayer for Spiritual Breakthrough.* Ventura, CA: Regal Books, 1997.

Vine, W.E. *The Expanded Vine's Expository Dictionary of New Testament Words.* Minneapolis: Bethany House Publishers, 1984.

Wagner, C. Peter. *Prayer Shield.* Ventura, CA: Regal Books, 1992.

Wentroble, Barbara. *Praying with Authority.* Ventura, CA: Regal Books, 2003.

Whyte, H.A. Maxwell. *The Kiss of Satan.* Monroeville, PA: Whitaker House, 1973.

Other Books by
Dr. Patti Amsden

The Law of Boundaries

Discover the principles through which you may become a faithful steward in tending that which is within your boundary without breaking the No Trespassing signs that God has posted throughout His creation. Special attention is given to the 10 Commandments as the Scripture's preeminent boundary laws.

The Apostles' Creed

One of the historic creeds of the church, The Apostles' Creed declares a blueprint from creation to consummation. It is a synopsis of historic faith and biblical truth that the church fathers fought to protect. This book will help you to discover the continuity of God's plan for the ages.

Evidence That Calls Us to Dance

Mankind is designed to express his story visually. This book examines biblical passages and scientific studies to present abundant evidence that God has structured all things in elaborately-choreographed and perfectly-metered dance. All creation tells its story through movement.

Patti Amsden Ministry
1203 Vandalia
Collinsville, Illinois 62234
Phone: 618-345-4224, Ext. 109
www.pattiamsden.org